Benjamin West

ALLEGORY AND ALLEGIANCE

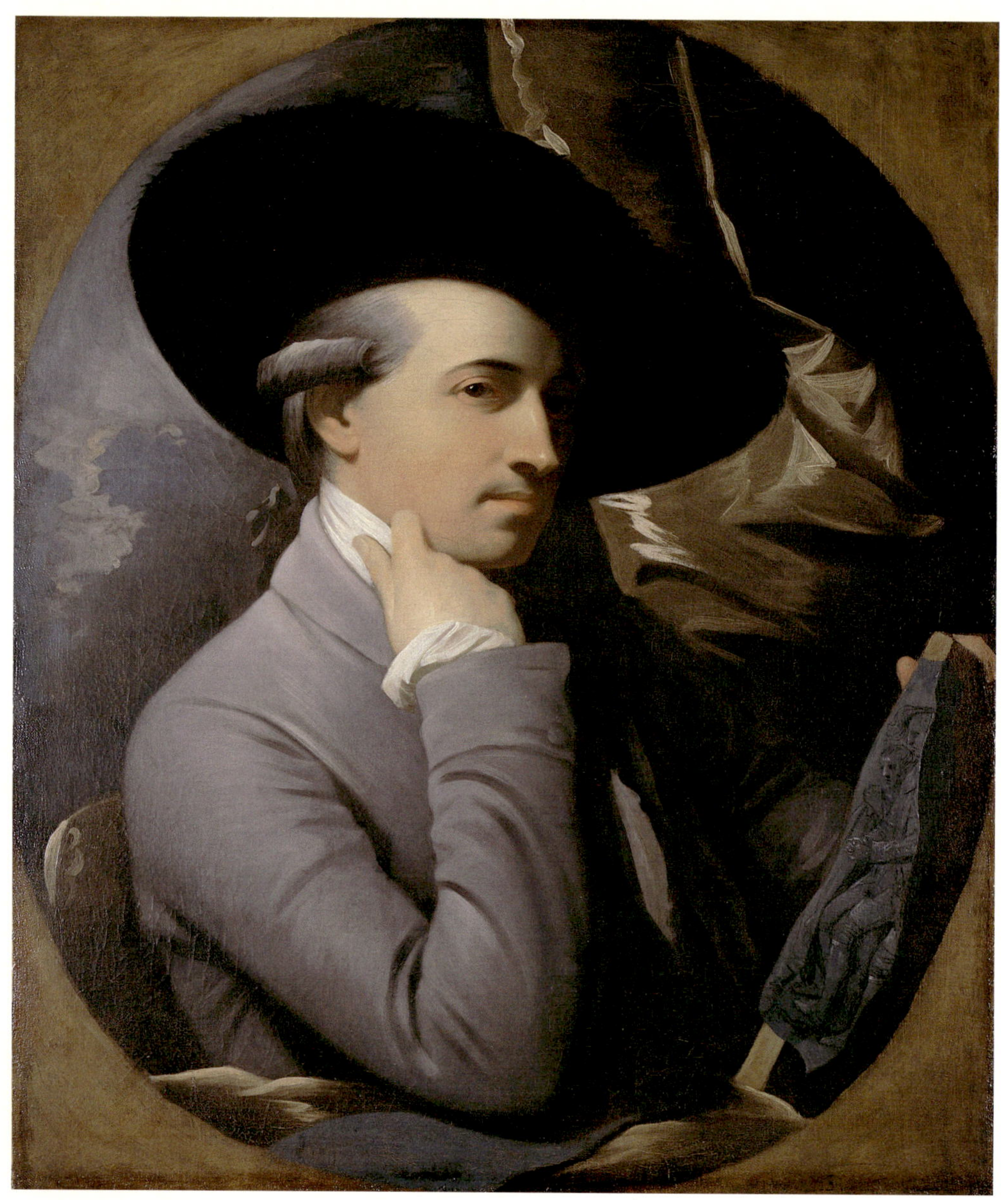

Benjamin West, *Self-Portrait,* c. 1770–76

Oil on canvas. The Baltimore Museum of Art: Gift of Dr. Morton K. Blaustein, Barbara B. Hirschhorn, and Elizabeth B. Roswell, in memory of Jacob and Hilda K. Blaustein, BMA 1981.73

Derrick R. Cartwright

Benjamin West

ALLEGORY AND ALLEGIANCE

TIMKEN MUSEUM OF ART • SAN DIEGO, CALIFORNIA

This catalogue accompanies the exhibition of the same name, presented at the Timken Museum of Art, November 5, 2004–February 27, 2005.

Distributed by the University of Washington Press, P.O. Box 50096, Seattle, WA 98145

ISBN: 1-879067-08-0

Library of Congress Control Number: 2004114665

COVER: Benjamin West, *Fidelia and Speranza* (detail), catalogue 1

EDITORS: Judith Dunham and Fronia W. Simpson
PROOFREADER: Kristina Youso
DESIGN: Gordon Chun Design

Printed by Hatcher Press, San Carlos, California

CONTENTS

LENDERS TO THE EXHIBITION

Friends Historical Library, Swarthmore College, Swarthmore, Pennsylvania

Hood Museum of Art, Dartmouth College, Hanover, New Hampshire

The Montreal Museum of Fine Arts, Montreal

Wadsworth Atheneum, Hartford, Connecticut

Yale Center for British Art, New Haven, Connecticut

CONTRIBUTORS TO THE EXHIBITION

FRIENDS OF THE TIMKEN
THE PUTNAM FOUNDATION

Dr. Charles C. and Sue K. Edwards
Sally Stevens Jones
Dr. Michael and Marilyn Kelley
Sharon and Joel Labovitz
Rita and Josiah Neeper
Jesse Osuna
Therese Truitt Whitcomb

Faiya and Milton Fredman
Mary Ann and Arnold Ginnow
Don and Celeste Hillman
Mr. and Mrs. William R. MacKenzie
Mrs. Richard C. Mitchell
The J. Douglas and Marian R. Pardee Foundation
Lisa and Richard Zinne

Charles H. Cutter
Mrs. Robert H. Davis
Madeline L. Goldberg
Ingrid B. Hibben
Anne Hoehn
Ruth F.C. Johnson
Mr. and Mrs. Thomas Ladner
Mr. and Mrs. Bernadotte Lester
Glenn Mosier
Mr. and Mrs. Philip R. Palisoul
Mary Lou Peterson
Dr. and Mrs. R. Edward Sanchez
Mr. and Mrs. Fred C. Stalder
Mr. and Mrs. John Thiele
Dixie and Ken Unruh
Victor and Gilda Vilaplana
Robert and Ginger Wallace
Mrs. Thomas R. Wilkinson

FOREWORD

The Timken Museum of Art showcases the history of European painting through works of Italian, Spanish, Dutch, Flemish, and French origin, as well as American paintings of the eighteenth and nineteenth centuries that reveal the development of European painting traditions in the New World. Whether by design, taste, or the vagaries of the market and fashion, visitors will not find within our galleries examples of British art. For the likes of Gainsborough, Constable, Turner, and Hogarth, visitors must go elsewhere.

Nevertheless, the Putnam Foundation's ties to England run deep. Several of the Foundation's most prized paintings, including those of Bartolomeo Veneto, Veronese, and Guercino, once graced the walls of Britain's stately homes. Rembrandt's *St. Bartholomew* formed part of the collection of Sir Joshua Reynolds, the preeminent portraitist and history painter of eighteenth-century England and the first president of the Royal Academy of Arts.

The connections grow even deeper and certainly more complex when the Putnam Foundation's American holdings are brought into consideration. Eastman Johnson's quintessentially American depiction of the cranberry harvest, painted in 1880, resided unrecorded in a private English collection for more than seventy years. *Mrs. Thomas Gage*, painted by John Singleton Copley, the greatest artist of eighteenth-century America, hung at Firle Place, the Gage family estate outside London, until its acquisition by the Putnam Foundation.

This interplay grows ever richer when one contemplates the respective careers of Copley and his contemporary Benjamin West. Copley and West were born in America in the same year, 1738, and both chose to pursue their careers in England. Unlike Copley, who was an already established artist when he departed for England just before the onset of the Revolutionary War, West was only twenty-two when he left America. He would spend virtually his entire career in England, becoming, at thirty-four, historical painter to George III and achieving great success as a portraitist and history painter.

Benjamin West: Allegory and Allegiance explores the complexities of an American-born artist whose success in London coincided with America's struggle for independence from England. Drawing on recent scholarship, Derrick R. Cartwright, guest scholar for this exhibition, artfully argues for a new, more profound appreciation of West, the difficulties that his dual allegiances must have engendered, and the three paintings with Spenserian subjects that West is known to have produced in the 1770s. We are very grateful to Derrick for undertaking this provocative and at times daunting enterprise.

Thanks to the generosity of our lenders, for the first time in more than two centuries the Timken's *Fidelia and Speranza* can now be seen in its Spenserian context, alongside *Una and the Lion* and *The Cave of Despair,* as well as preparatory drawings and prints based on these paintings.

For their support of this project we would like to thank the following institutions and individuals: Yale Center for British Art—Amy Meyers and Timothy Goodhue; Wadsworth Atheneum—Willard Holmes, Betsy Kornhauser, Mary Herbert Busick, and Andrew Fotta; Friends Historical Library, Swarthmore College—Christopher Densmore; Hood Museum of Art—Barbara J. MacAdam, Kellen Haak, and Kathleen O'Malley; and the Montreal Museum of Fine Arts—Guy Cogeval, Danielle Archambault, Simon Labrie, and Linda-Anne D'Anjou. We are especially indebted to Fronia W. Simpson and Judith Dunham for their editorial efforts, and to Suzanne and Gordon Chun for the design of this catalogue.

Finally, we offer a special thanks to the Friends of the Timken. It is through their annual contributions that projects such as *Benjamin West: Allegory and Allegiance* are made possible.

John A. Petersen
Executive Director

Hal Fischer
Director of Exhibitions and Publications

PREFACE

This essay began as an informal talk titled "Benjamin West's *Fidelia and Speranza* (1776): Another Kind of Declaration of Independence?" delivered at the Timken Museum of Art in 1997. I thank Nancy Ames Petersen, former director of the Timken, and Gay Michal Nay, director of education, first and foremost, for having invited me to speak. Afterward, John Petersen expressed his belief that West's elusive painting might add to the admirable series of focus exhibitions produced around major works in the Timken's permanent collection. John has been unstinting in his support of this project and I extend my lasting gratitude to him, and to the directors of the Putnam Foundation, in these acknowledgments.

Hal Fischer played an instrumental role in the completion of this exhibition. He supervised all aspects of the exhibition and catalogue and pursued me as I crossed and recrossed the continent while completing the essay that follows. His impact has been considerable, therefore. Judith Dunham copyedited the text and Fronia W. Simpson insisted on greater precision in many of its arguments. I am deeply grateful to these editors for their efforts, their art historical expertise, and their patience. Amy Meyers, Director of the Yale Center for British Art, was, as always, a generous and helpful colleague. Angus Trumble, Curator of Paintings and Sculpture, provided ready access to the essential files in New Haven. Malcolm Warner, Chief Curator of the Kimbell Museum of Art, challenged and encouraged many of the concepts that stand behind this exhibition at the moment of their formation. Barbara J. MacAdam, Curator of American Art at the Hood Museum of Art, Dartmouth College, kindly read a version of the catalogue essay on a last-minute basis and offered substantive feedback.

I confess that I am myself neither a scholar of British literature nor a specialist in late-eighteenth-century American painting. My curiosity about West's *Faerie Queene* pictures has been driven, just the same, by a belief that cross-disciplinary efforts in museums can yield insights that more purely art historical approaches tend only to conceal. Whatever flaws there are to the speculative approach demonstrated here should be traced back to their author, but not to the underlying promise of methodological experiments. I am reminded of how fortunate I have been to have had many extraordinary teachers who, in reading this text, may recognize their shaping influence upon it. Certainly I am indebted to Margaretta Lovell, Joel Isaacson, Marc Simpson, James Cuno, Alan Wallach, and the late David Huntingon for the many scholarly gifts they offered me. Finally, I wish to thank my family—Lauren, Sarah, Julia, and Graham—for the prominent place they represent in all of my creative efforts.

Derrick R. Cartwright

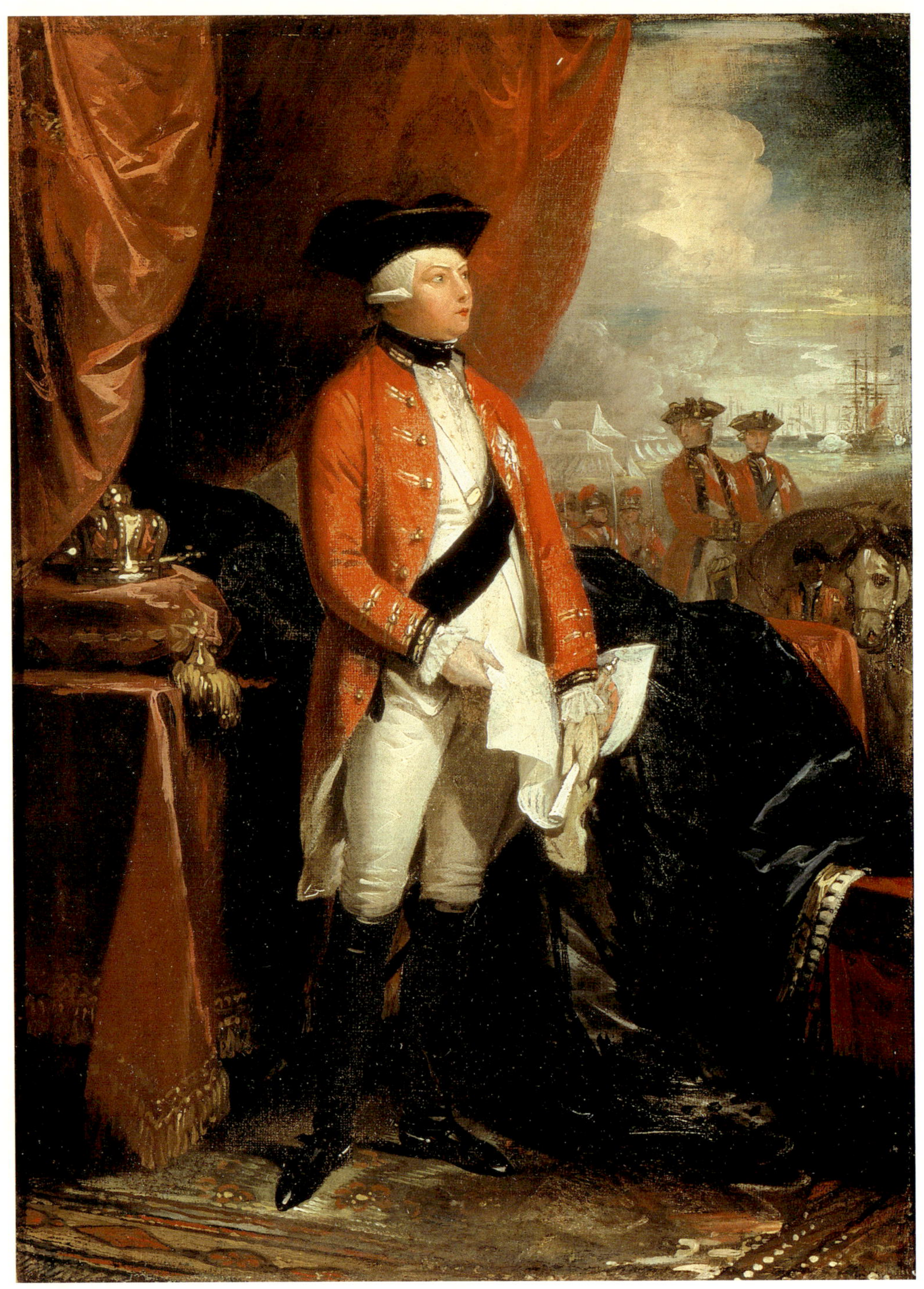

FIG. 1. Benjamin West, *King George III (1738–1820)*, c. 1779

Oil on canvas. Courtesy of Historical Society of Pennsylvania Collection, Atwater Kent Museum of Philadelphia / Bridgeman Art Library

Allegory and Allegiance in Benjamin West's Spenserian Subjects

Derrick R. Cartwright

At the outset of the most ambitious phase of his career, American-born painter Benjamin West (1738–1820; frontispiece) turned his attention to the allegorical poetry of Edmund Spenser (c. 1552–99). His dedication to this literary subject matter was intense but short-lived, and he kept whatever motives he had for pursuing Spenser private. As a result, West's works based on the English poet's writing are not well known today. The artist is best remembered instead for his large-scale, grand manner history paintings, many developed as royal commissions.

West had lived in London for not quite five years when George III (1738–1820; fig. 1) took notice of him, in 1768. The artist first attracted the king's attention with narrative paintings in a morally instructive, coloristically restrained, yet highly theatrical neoclassical style. *Agrippina Landing at Brundisium with the Ashes of Germanicus* (fig. 2), for example, with its severe procession of mourning figures moving across a stagelike architectural space and its high intellectual pretensions, caused a sensation among London audiences. The notoriety of the work may have facilitated the founding of the Royal Academy that same year. Soon after that promising work was completed, George III commissioned West to produce a related history painting, which was highly celebrated. About four years after that, West was appointed historical painter to the king.[1] Less than a decade later, West was named the second president of the Royal Academy of Arts, succeeding his longtime rival Sir Joshua Reynolds.

West's sudden, royally sanctioned ascendancy was unprecedented. At roughly the same time that he embarked on his major contributions to neoclassical history painting, the artist produced a series of pictures based on Spenser's *The Faerie Queene* (1590, 1596). Beginning in the seventeenth century, Spenser's verse provided an increasingly steady flow of imagery for English narrative painting, sculpture, and illustration. West was among the first academic painters to approach this notoriously complex allegory. The culmination of his involvement with the epic is the large, striking, and enigmatic *Fidelia and Speranza* (cat. 1). The composition shows two delicately elongated female figures standing arm in arm in a cavelike space. The women are unmistakable symbols of linked virtues, Faith and Hope, an identification that is clinched in Spenser's text. The painting's underlying message, however, is unclear.

As rigorously developed allegories, both Spenser's poem and West's pictures based on it beg to be read on multiple levels. Did *Fidelia and Speranza* have symbolic meaning for West in 1776, the year that he chose this literary subject? This essay addresses the question by probing the personal, historical, and pictorial circumstances surrounding West's immersion in *The Faerie Queene*. It points toward external sources—in the artist's contemporary historical context and in past and present literary responses—as well as to the internal structure of the works themselves for clues to their complex meanings. This essay suggests that West's investigation of this unwieldy Elizabethan text represented a commitment to certain ideas that suited him as an ambitious artist. He looked to Spenser for an example of personally virtuous and historically validated English creativity—a model against which he might test his rising stature within the British court of the 1770s and his enduring allegiance to his North American heritage during the years of the American Revolution.

On one level, West's devotion to *The Faerie Queene* can be measured by the time he committed to the overall project—about a decade and a half—and the number of independent finished works in oil—three. Such quantification, however, makes the endeavor seem attenuated

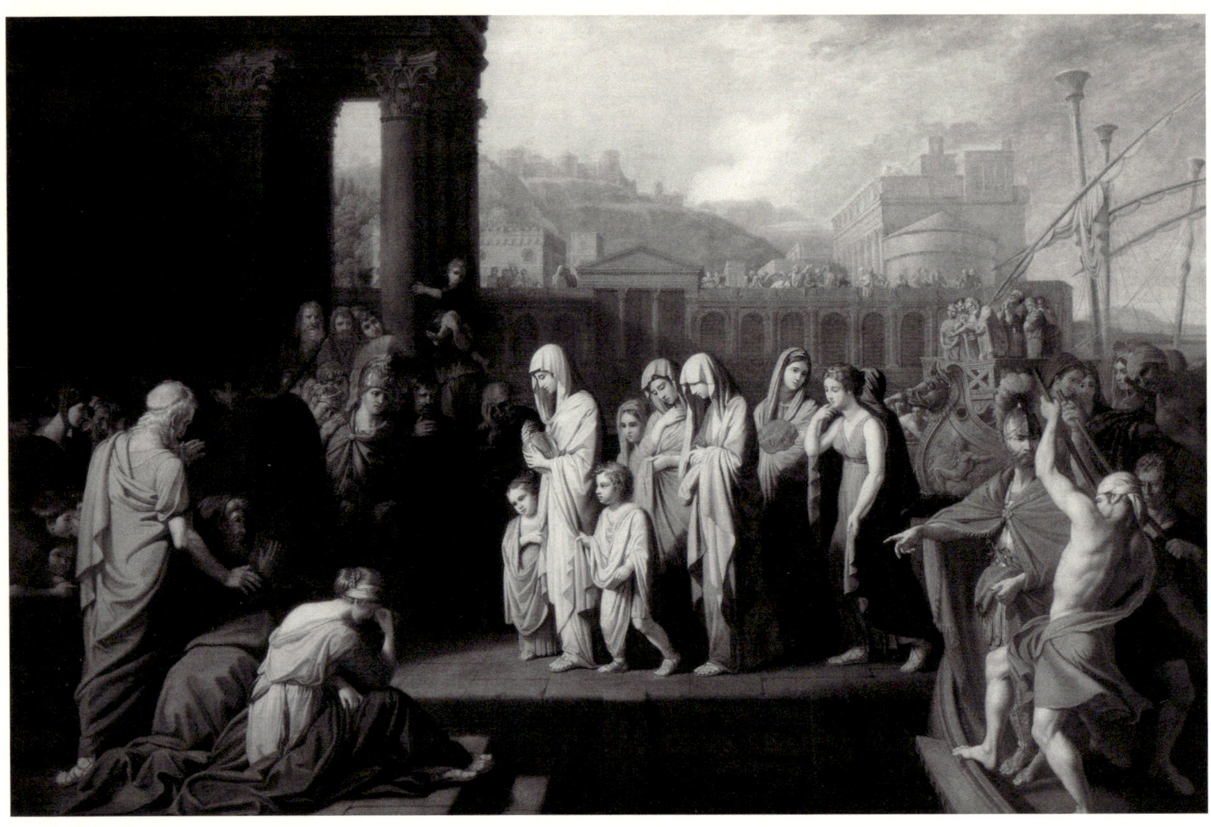

FIG. 2. Benjamin West, *Agrippina Landing at Brundisium with the Ashes of Germanicus*, 1768
Oil on canvas. Yale University Art Gallery, Gift of Louis M. Rabinowitz, 1947.16

and slight. Accordingly, scholars have relegated the artist's interest in Spenser to a marginal status within an otherwise long, varied, and unpredictable career. The images have been recorded in catalogues, and they are mentioned from time to time in monographic studies, but they have not inspired much in the way of celebration or revisionism.[2] Like other aspects of West's oeuvre, these works are not treated with the seriousness that recent art historians accord to other major painting enterprises of the late eighteenth century.[3] This is a common problem when it comes to West. The artist was characterized as possessing a "private life [that] was like an open book," resulting in a tendency to treat his overall contributions in superficial terms. Recontextualizing the principal works in this series allows us to trace West's intricate, allegorical approach to *The Faerie Queene* series to their source. Allegory provided West with safe, if coded, means to make controversial assertions against reigning authorities—both peers and monarchs—that might otherwise have inhibited his rising status. In no other single work is this so challengingly demonstrated than in *Fidelia and Speranza*.

A brief survey of West's biography establishes a basis for reinterpreting the Spenserian images in fresh terms. West was the son of a British-born Quaker, John West, a onetime cooper turned tavern keeper. Born in Springfield Township (now Swarthmore), Pennsylvania, West was the youngest child in a large family. He demonstrated a prodigious talent for drawing before the age of ten.[4] Little is known about his youthful training in art except for his report of contact with British-born artist William Williams, perhaps as early as 1747.[5] West took art lessons from Moravian preacher and itinerant painter John Valentine

Haidt about 1754.[6] While still a teenager, he painted his first known history painting, *The Death of Socrates* (1756, private collection), a work that scholars rightly call "awkward but ambitious."[7] He adapted that work from an engraved frontispiece to the fourth volume of Charles Rollin's epic text, *Ancient History*.[8] From early on, then, West borrowed ideas from authoritative texts to create heroic compositions. More than this, by choosing to make a historical painting, he demonstrated a keen awareness of the genre's growing importance. In mid-eighteenth-century Pennsylvania, portraiture appealed to a relatively limited public interested in likenesses for the purpose of demonstrating new personal wealth and securing intergenerational, interfamilial links. In England, "face-pictures," "conversation groups," and landscapes were the dominant representations. There, and in America, history painting lacked the status it enjoyed in Continental Europe since the seventeenth century. Therefore, West's practice of history painting as a colonial youth speaks volumes about his early self-consciousness and ambition.

Educated elites in Philadelphia and New York embraced the young artist, though West had virtually no claims to being an intellectual himself. In the 1750s he gravitated toward Pennsylvania's urban center, where he quickly won support from prominent men, including the Reverend William Smith, Justice William Allen, and Lieutenant Governor James Hamilton. The three played roles in encouraging the artist to visit Europe, a study trip that they ultimately financed and from which West never returned. With the help of these benefactors, he voyaged from Philadelphia to Livorno, on Italy's Ligurian coast, in April 1760. West spent a bit more than three years in Italy, carrying letters of introduction that boasted of his raw artistic ability. By July 1761 he had reached Rome and stayed there until November. During those first months he had audiences with the principal artistic authorities of the day—Cardinal Alessandro Albani and Johann Joachim Winckelmann, in particular—who were as much amused as they were impressed by the North American prodigy.

Scholars often retell the story of West's first untutored confrontation with the Apollo Belvedere at the Vatican, an image that the young American is said to have likened to a "Mohawk warrior," to the incredulity of his Italian hosts.[9] The comparison was calculated and, though shocking, endeared West to his Italian entourage. The event became a lasting component of his personal mythology and appears in virtually every treatment of the artist's life. The encounter calls for a deeper interpretation, however. If accurate, it shows West's adeptness at turning threatening encounters with cultural elites into new relationships and also indicates his refusal to acknowledge any presumed feelings of inferiority. Furthermore, West never forgot the hybrid illusion of Native American and god of culture, for the pose appears repeatedly as a recognizable citation throughout his work. This was only the first of many shrewdly considered allegorical substitutions put forward by the young artist.

While still in Italy, West established a coterie of respected peers, among them Anton Raphael Mengs, Gavin Hamilton, Angelica Kauffmann, and Pompeo Batoni.[10] He followed their advice by copying works of Renaissance masters such as Titian and Correggio and then by familiarizing himself with recommended literary sources. Mengs pointed West toward classic Italian texts. West created the first of his literary pictures toward the very end of his sojourn. *Cymon and Iphegenia* (1763) was based on Giovanni Boccaccio's *The Decameron* as well as on John Dryden's popular, contemporary theatrical revival of the fourteenth-century narrative.[11]

After completing that now lost picture, West looked next to Spenser's precursor in epic poetry, Ludovico Ariosto. *Orlando Furioso,* published in 1516 and first translated into English in 1591, provided him with the subject of *Angelica and Medoro* (fig. 3).[12] He began the picture in Rome and carried it with him in an unfinished form to London in late 1763. The work tells the story of a beautiful young princess, Angelica, who falls hopelessly in love with a Moorish youth, Medoro. It was likely intended as a pendant to *Cymon and Ipheginia. Angelica and Medoro* has also been interpreted as a coded personal reference to his close friend, Swiss painter Angelica Kauffmann.[13] The personal nature of such an homage is significant. The painting can be seen as a private declaration of West's amorous interest, a

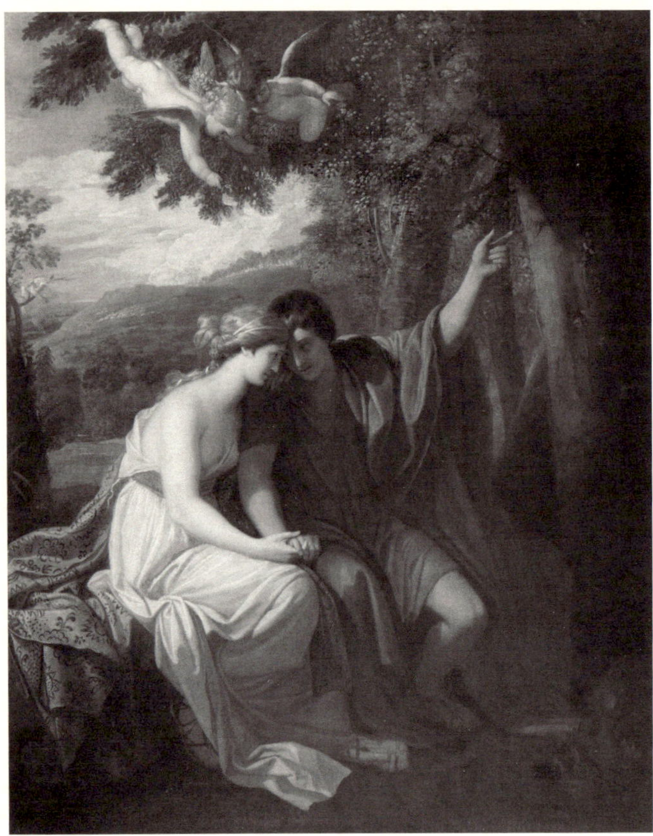

FIG. 3. Benjamin West, *Angelica and Medoro,* 1764–65
Oil on canvas. Binghamton University Art Museum, Binghamton, New York, 1969.12

reading supported by his self-allegorization as the conspicuous foreigner Medoro. The work stands as another example of West's deepening interest in the potential use of allegory in his art.

West was in England for the first time in August 1763, stopping briefly in France en route. London was planned as a rest stop on the way back to America, but it became the artist's permanent home instead. Building on the discovery of allegorical sources that he had begun in Italy, West quickly recognized "the British penchant for verbal rather than visual gratification."[14] British artists were already well regarded as portraitists and, from the eighteenth century, as landscapists, but they were not nearly so highly esteemed as painters of history or literary subjects. English logic promoted ideas above things, and painters consequently occupied a low place in the hierarchy of the arts.[15] Within the span of West's British career, however, a dramatic shift took place. In the 1760s he exploited a prevailing taste for literature by creating a wide variety of narrative pictures. This continued throughout his nearly six decades of practice in England.

The sources for West's paintings from the early years of George III's reign reflect his unexpectedly diverse literary sensibility: Shakespeare, Dryden, Ariosto, the Bible, and Edmund Spenser. Major paintings from these first years in London promote the artist's newly acquired interest in the heroic nude form—*Hercules between Virtue and Vice* (1764, Victoria and Albert Museum), for example—and his indebtedness to antique statuary. Both West's official portraits and his private works demonstrate his taste for highbrow associations. A family portrait (fig. 4) shows his emulation of Raphael as much as it achieves an intensely close portrayal of mother and the artist's first child, who was named after the Renaissance master. The subjects are bound figuratively and emotionally, and by their gaze connecting them with the artist. This private image predicts future compositions pairing subjects of closely held significance.

In 1766 West won praise for two neoclassical works exhibited at the Society of Arts exhibition: *Pylades and Orestes Brought as Victims before Ipheginia* (1766, Tate Gallery, London) and *The Continence of Scipio* (c. 1766, Fitzwilliam Museum of Art, Cambridge). After this, however, epic poetry began to compete directly with history painting as a favored subject. West painted five different versions of *Rinaldo and Armida* (fig. 5), a popular scene from Torquino Tasso's *Gerusalemme Liberata* (1575). Tasso, along with Ariosto, was a favorite of Spenser's. The works of both had been read in translation by the British public since the seventeenth century and by audiences in North America in West's time.[16]

The readiness with which West approached these cultivated literary references is even more remarkable when considering his lack of background. As the Apollo Belvedere episode revealed, West never perceived his practical naïveté as a hindrance. His involvement with *The Faerie Queene* became an epic demonstration of his effort to use allegorical literature for the purpose of forging a meaningful new role for himself as an artist even as he experienced competing crises of conscience and allegiance. West was drawn back and forth between his historical subject choices and their potential allegorical intersections with his past. In the 1770s this meant that he pointed indirectly at North America in works done for his English clientele and, most important, for the king. As the colonies began to rebel against British taxation and military occupation, West's focus was unquestionably laden with mixed emotions and even partisanship.

Confirming this, a search for North American themes in West's work at the outset of his English residency yields a larger inventory than might be expected. He produced several drawings of Native Americans that were reproduced as engravings in books dedicated to New World subjects (fig. 6).[17] While these miniatures deliberately recall events that took place as recently as 1764, they also subtly reference well-known ancient prototypes, such as the Apollo Belvedere and Trajan's Column. Jules Prown has convincingly argued that these works offered West opportunities to create "visual sources that would enable him to continue his artistic analogizing between classical antiquity and the present."[18] These works, though ostensibly minor, might be said to represent an important transitional impulse in an emerging personal aesthetic. More significant, they could be considered allegories in their own right.

Before becoming an established figure in the art world of Britain, West developed a clear interest in Old World cultural prototypes combined with conspicuously contemporary references, especially if he could make these forms relevant to his New World mythmaking. Allegory provided a mechanism for making multiple statements through a single image. West fully exploited this potential in substantial works in all genres, such as the violent historical canvas *General Johnson Saving a Wounded French Officer from the Tomohawk of a North American Indian* (c. 1764–68, Derby Museum and Art Gallery) and the recollected landscape *View on the Susquehanna River* (1767, Henry Francis du Pont Winterthur Museum). West's stately, full-sized portrait *General Robert Monckton* (c. 1764, Trustees of Lady Galway's Chattels Settlement, London), a colonial governor

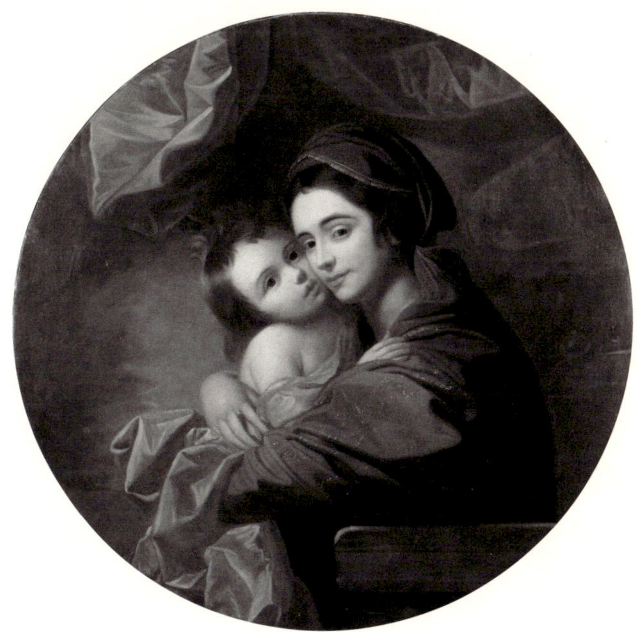

FIG. 4. Benjamin West, *Mrs. West with Raphael West,* c. 1770
Oil on canvas. From the permanent collection of the Utah Museum of Fine Arts, Acc.1982.007.003

and war hero of the French American campaign, celebrated heroic deeds, regional splendor, and the artist's evolving reputation for setting classically based compositions within North American environments.

In all these subjects, West deliberately flaunted his disregard for many recently established practices in British art, and to an equal degree, he put his brush on a political sore spot. Resistance to new British taxation in 1764 and 1765 and street violence in Boston in 1768 were indisputable precursors to broader conflict in the colonies. West's predilection for conspicuously North American scenes called attention to him as a colonial subject. Professional and personal resistance to this stance on the part of his English audiences, while hard to measure now, had legendary effects. At least one masterpiece by West, *The Death of General Wolfe,* was the outcome of this productive tension.

The Death of General Wolfe (fig. 7) represented a breakthrough in West's artistic career and also signaled an impending crisis. James Wolfe's name was inextricably tied to the British victory over the French at the Battle of Quebec in mid-September 1759, a pivotal episode in the French and Indian War. That war, fought in essence to

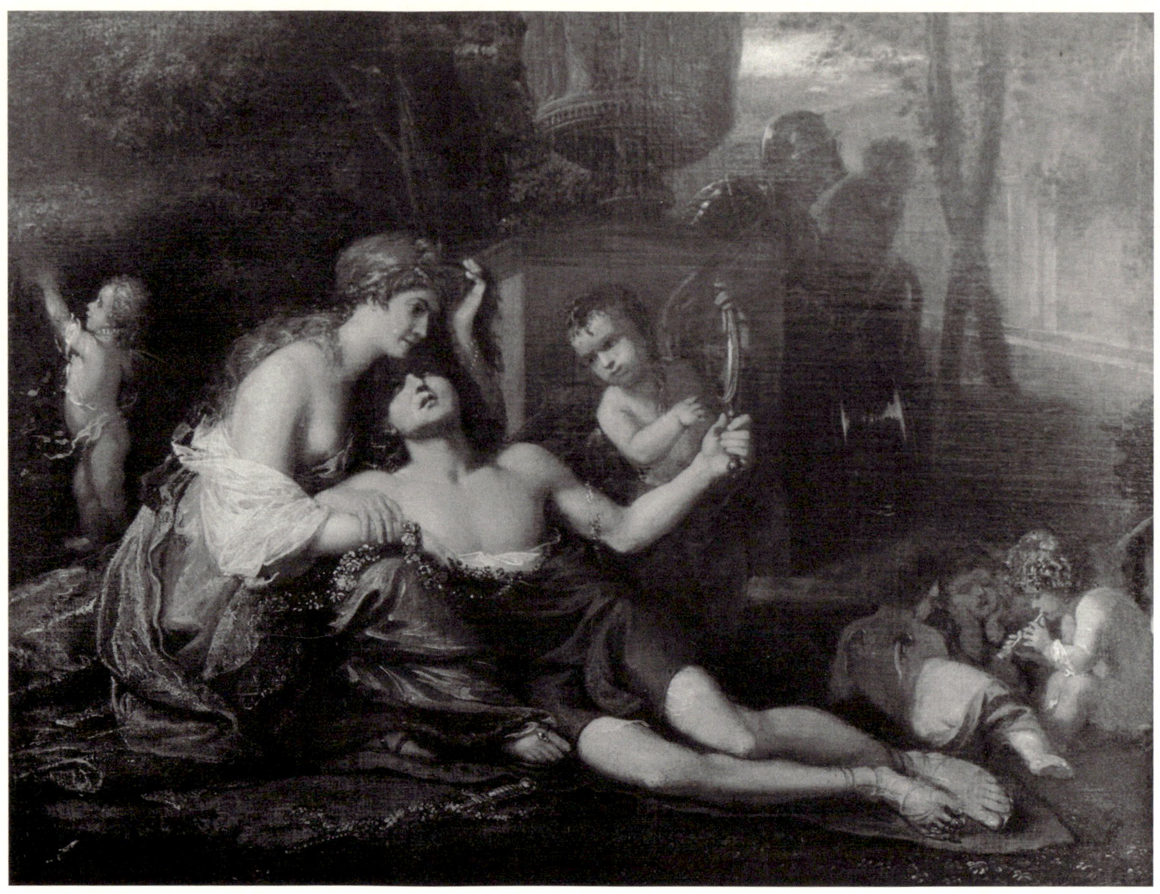

FIG. 5. Benjamin West, *Rinaldo and Armida,* 1766

Oil on canvas. Jane Voorhees Zimmerli Art Museum, Rutgers, The State University of New Jersey, Gift of Willet L. Eccles. Photo: Jack Abraham

expand British dominion in North America, had the effect of increasing civic unrest after a peace treaty was signed in 1763. New taxes on colonial subjects were the result. A decade after the battle, General Wolfe's valor remained part of a common memory, but the location and consequences may have receded slightly from public consciousness. In his potent military homage, West insists as much on geographic specificity and allegorical meaning as on heroic portraiture. The painting shows the dying British war hero in the attitude of a Renaissance Pietà, encircled by admirers, including General Monckton and a prominently placed Native American. The painting visually, historically, and rhetorically links the abstract ideal of sacrifice and the place of sacrifice.

The American artist's decision to treat the momentous and morally instructive historical scene in contemporary terms was an issue even before the painting's first public exhibition. The notion was called into question by Sir Joshua Reynolds, who on seeing the work in a still unfinished state remarked that its "unorthodoxy would imperil the growing reputation of art in this country." That statement characterized West's contribution in terms of rebellion. Reynolds counseled West to adopt instead "the classic costume of antiquity as much more becoming the inherent greatness of his subject than the modern garb of war."[19] Famously, and also somewhat rebelliously, West dismissed the advice. He asserted that in their enlightened moment both he and Reynolds should observe that "the same truth which gives law to the historian should rule the painter."[20] This exchange—an aesthetic debate framed in terms of rebellion, contemporary historical awareness, and legal rights—shows how politically divisive aesthetic discussions in Britain had become. West's *Wolfe* received initial critical success in its showing at the Royal Academy in 1771, and Reynolds reversed his earlier critical stance, predicting that the picture would "occasion a revolution in the art."[21]

Exhibited in the academy's Pall Mall space (fig. 8), West's work drew avid praise. He received three orders for copies over the next ten years, including one version for the king, who had refused to consider the original due to Reynolds's deprecating remarks. *The Death of General Wolfe* was sent out for engraving by William Woollett.[22] The reproductive print was distributed in England, France, and North America, and brought financial rewards to the engraver, the publisher, John Boydell, and the artist. The idea that West might place a contemporary British general in the role of a religious martyr found an eager audience in England, even inspiring a satirical response from famed eighteenth-century caricaturist James Gillray. The work was vital for West because the sacrificial scene took place in North America. Vivien Green Fryd has argued that for those who could not immediately recognize the battlefield as the Plains of Abraham, the prominent placement of the Iroquois brave in the painting's lower left provided the key to the geographic specificity. Fryd further asserts that while the pose of the figure is clearly based on West's study of the Belvedere torso, "the Native American also adds an exotic, romantic element. He signifies the concept of *mirabilia,* replacing the remoteness in time found in traditional history paintings of the ancient world . . . with a remoteness of place, a faraway location such as the new world."[23] The muscular, tattooed Iroquois is the compositional and figurative counterpoint to the slack, uniformed body of Wolfe. The Native American pondering the nature of European cultural and political authorities merits empathy and could be seen as a substitute for West. The artist's penchant for pointedly rhetorical substitutions of this personal nature should not be underestimated.

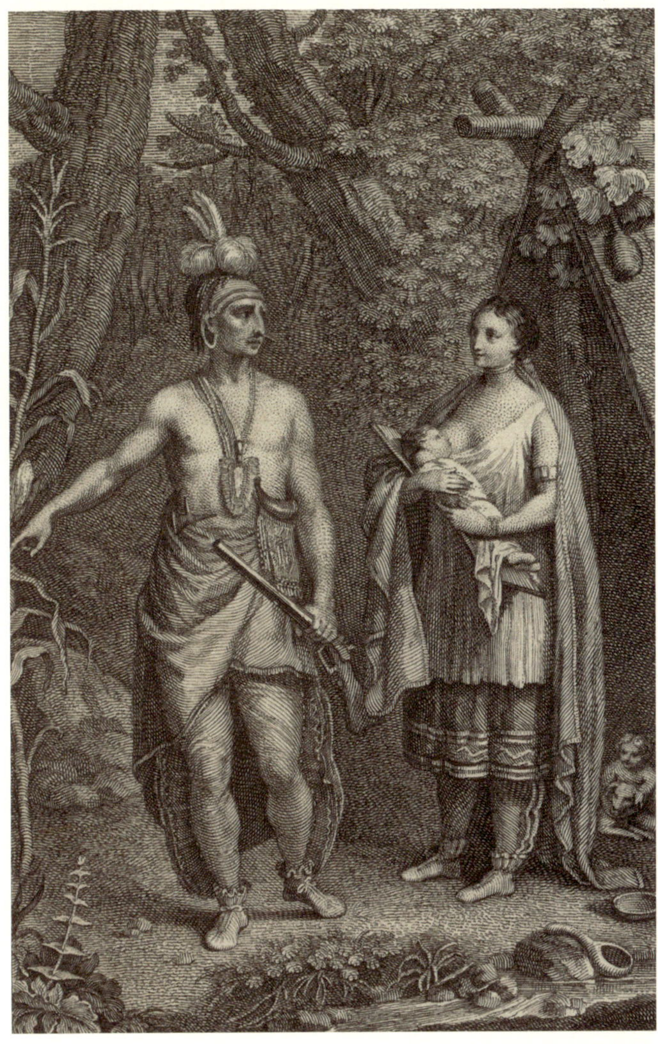

FIG. 6. Francesco Bartolozzi (after Benjamin West), *Savage Warrior Taking Leave of His Family*, 1763, engraving from Edmund Burke, *Account of European Settlement in America*

Courtesy of the Bancroft Library, University of California, Berkeley

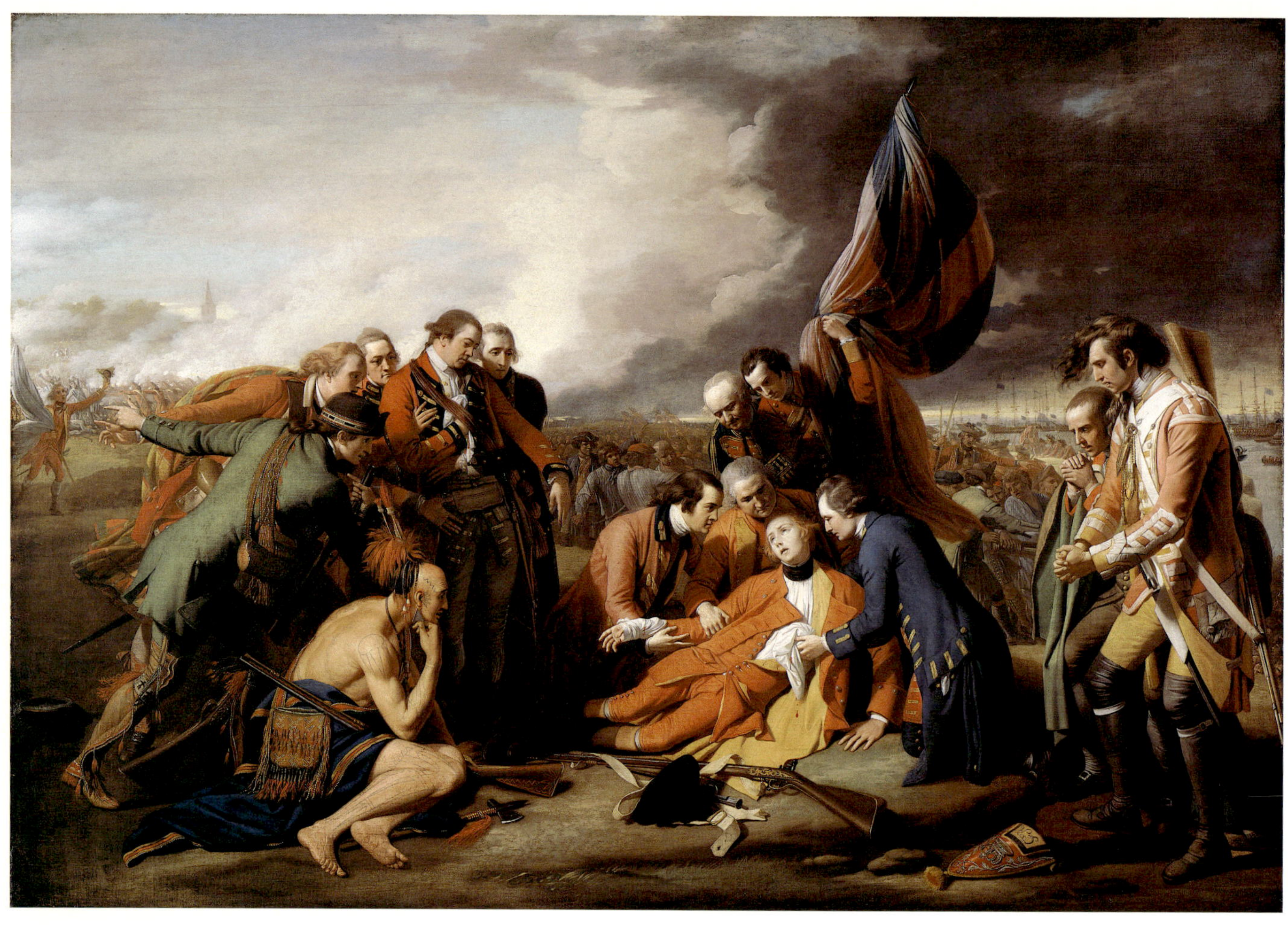

FIG. 7. Benjamin West, *The Death of General Wolfe,* 1770

Oil on canvas. National Gallery of Canada, Ottawa, Transfer from the Canadian War Memorials, 1921 (Gift of the 2nd Duke of Westminster, Eaton Hall, Cheshire, 1918)

In 1771—the year that *The Death of General Wolfe* signaled both his greatest original triumph as an artist to date and a conflicted attachment to his colonial roots—West embarked on a project that would provide him with an even more challenging set of historical and rhetorical substitutions: Spenser's *The Faerie Queene*. He could not have picked a better subject for rhetorical and pictorial exploration. Spenser's text allowed the artist to demonstrate a conflicted allegiance by proving his conscientiousness about and deference to the British origins of his subject while maintaining an identity that was at odds with that power.

The Faerie Queene is an elaborate, dense, highly ornamented, fundamentally incomplete text. As a result, it is, to a large degree, inaccessible for most twenty-first-century readers. Modern editions of the poem typically run to more than twelve hundred pages. The text is organized around the formal unit of the Spenserian stanza, a tour de force of poetic discipline, which imposes a rigid rhythmic structure. The meandering and inconsistent plot is virtually impossible for modern critics to summarize. *The Faerie Queene* represented a parallel world—a Fairyland—presided over by a benevolent regent, Gloriana, whose reign is defended by chivalrous heroes against a wide variety of evil forces. In concept, the poem aspired to provide a "morall example" of Christian virtues through independent, but "continued" allegories related throughout twelve books divided into multiple cantos. Spenser began work on the manuscript that would become *The Faerie Queene* as early as the 1580s. He completed only six of the twelve planned books during his lifetime. A seventh book was pieced together posthumously from available fragments and published in the early 1600s. As the first self-conscious epic written in the English language, the unfinished text bears special significance as a choice for pictorial representation. Any consideration of West's emerging interest in this source must first take into account what was unique to *The Faerie Queene*'s Renaissance context and what was notable about its revival in the mid-eighteenth century by artists.

Edmund Spenser was born about 1552 (fig. 9).[24] Like West, he emerged from an inauspicious social background to become a public figure of extraordinary cultural significance for England. Although he received a Cambridge education, Spenser only did so as the beneficiary of overmastering philanthropic forces that singled out his youthful talents and promoted his modest achievements with enthusiasm. After Spenser studied at Pembroke College, the earl of Leicester employed him in London and then introduced him to the court of Elizabeth I in or about 1579 (fig. 10). His first celebrated work, *The Shepheardes Calendar,* published that year, included an allegorically disguised celebration of the Virgin Queen in its verbal descriptions and directly represented her on the page dedicated to the month of "Aprill."[25]

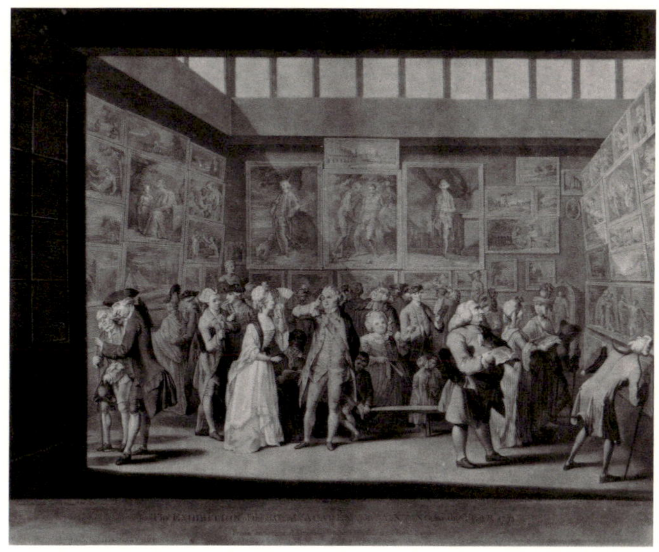

FIG. 8. Richard Earlom, after Michel Vincent Brandoin, *The Exhibition of the Royal Academy of Painting in the Year 1771,* 1772

Mezzotint. Hood Museum of Art, Dartmouth College, Hanover, NH; purchased through a gift from Jane and W. David Dance, Class of 1940. Copyright © Trustees of Dartmouth College, Hanover, New Hampshire. Photo: Jeffrey Nintzel

As a secretary to Arthur, Lord Grey de Wilton, Spenser traveled to Ireland, where he embraced a harsh political philosophy of English hegemony over an Irish population straining toward sovereignty. The poet's experiences in Ireland were formative. He wrote a controversial critique, *A view to the present state of Irelande* (1598). As a result, during his administrative service as clerk of the Council of Munster near Cork, Spenser likely first encountered Sir

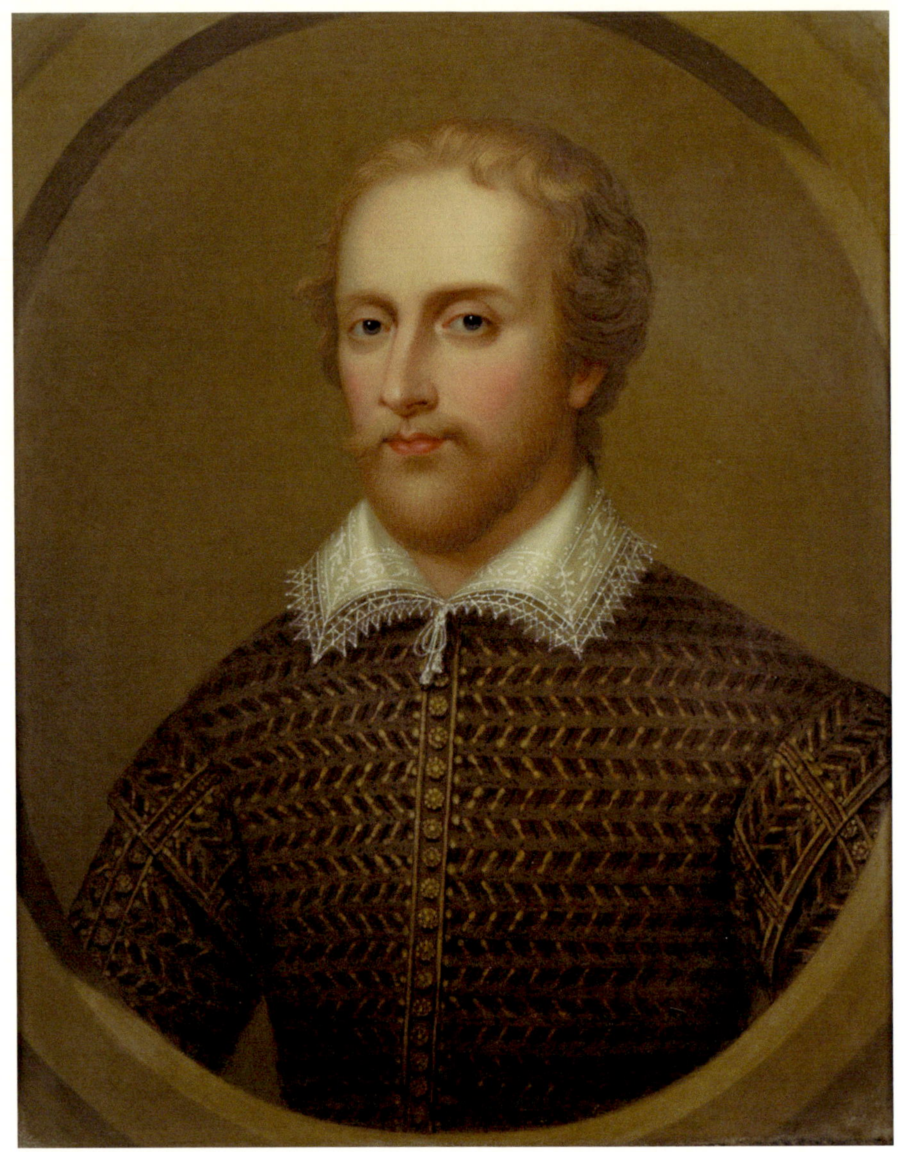

FIG. 9. Henry Bone, *Edmund Spenser (c. 1552–1599)*

Enamel on copper. Kingston Lacy, Dorset, UK / National Trust Photographic Library / Derrick E. Witty / Bridgeman Art Library

Walter Raleigh, who provided him with his most sustained, direct access to the queen. Spenser formally dedicated his magnum opus to Elizabeth in the 1590 edition and elaborated those dedications in subsequent versions of his text. Spenser provided Raleigh with an explication of *The Faerie Queene*'s logic in his "Letter of the Authors" written in 1589:

> In that Faery Queene I meane glory in my generall intention, but in my particular I conceiue the most excellent and glorious person of our soueriaine the Queene, and her kingdom in Faery Land. Yet in some places els, I doe otherwise shadow her. For considering heareth two persons, the one of the most royall Queene or Empresse, the other of a most virtuous and beautifull Lady.[26]

The instruction to "hear" two persons alerts the reader to a double meaning throughout the text. What the reader hears—or sees—is only one dimension of the poet's strategy; every character has a second or even a third "voice" to which the reader must also be sensitive. Furthermore, the notion of "shadowing" connotes a different dynamic—something indirect, perhaps even covert. West borrowed these concepts from Spenser for use in his paintings.

Raleigh and Spenser were just two among many sixteenth-century courtiers actively competing for Elizabeth's patronage and affection. Spenser's ambitious rise within the court of Elizabeth thus mirrors West's aspiring relationship to George III roughly two centuries later. Just as West was rewarded with royal commissions and financial remuneration—ultimately receiving an annual stipend of £1,000 for his service—Spenser began receiving a stipend of £50 from the Tudors shortly after his first public accolades, in February 1591. This recognition came just a year after the first three books of his epic romance were printed. Given the timing, it is hard not to make a connection between *The Faerie Queene*'s publication and the reward for allegiance. Shortly afterward, Spenser was named poet laureate by the queen. With these venal attachments came expectations of devotion, which, in turn, created strains on the creative artist.

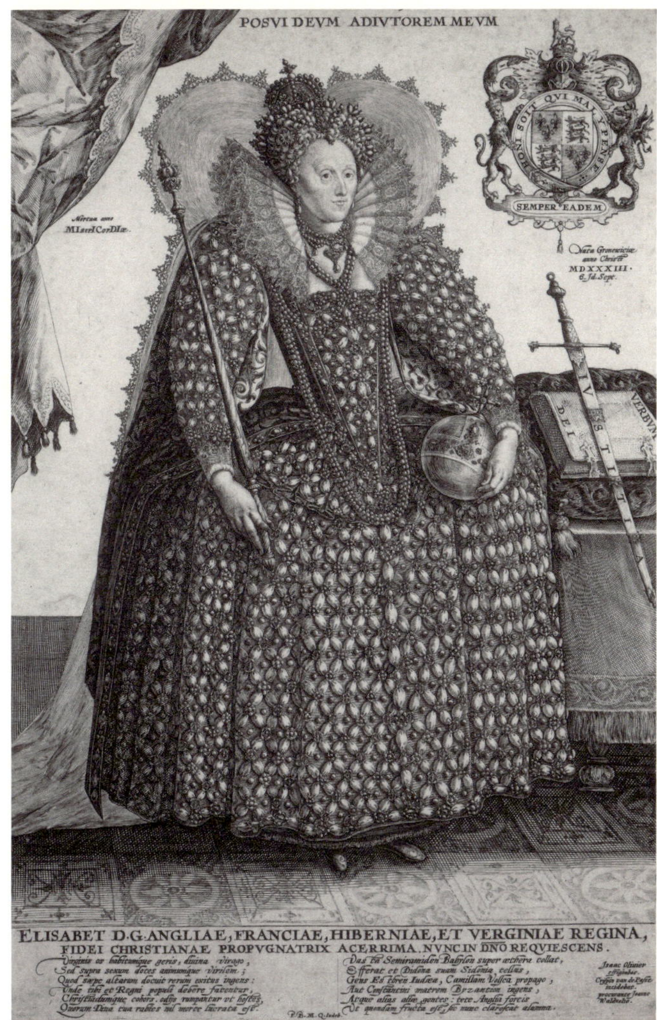

FIG. 10. Crispijn de Passe I, *Elizabeth, Queen of England*

Engraving. National Gallery of Art, Washington, Rosenwald Collection, 1943.3.6732.(PR)

Literary historians have argued that Spenser's work belongs to a special genre in which the panegyric form of the poem and its dedications masked deeper "disillusionment"—literally, shadows on the queen's glory. According to Susan Doran, *The Faerie Queene* was understood to be a thinly veiled "critique of Elizabeth's rule despite its reputation as a celebration of Gloriana," who is to be understood as Elizabeth.[27] Like West, Spenser suffered a considerable setback in terms of favor at court during the last years of his life. His reputation, fortune, and pride dipped ruinously, and the former poet laureate died "for lake of bread" in a London poorhouse. It is impossible to imagine West drawn to Spenser's text out of recognition of such biographical parallels, some of which were not yet known in the 1770s, but he probably grasped a certain alienated kinship with Spenser by reading the poet's life story included in most editions of *The Faerie Queene* since the early seventeenth century.

From the beginning of the eighteenth century, Spenser enjoyed a strong revival of readership. The number of new anthologies and Spenser-inspired imitations and adaptations from this period has been painstakingly calculated at considerably more than three hundred works in print.[28] England's born-again taste for Spenser emerged from a renewed Elizabethanism in political and social affairs, a strategy that sought to conserve chivalric ideals from encroaching Enlightenment values. A parallel between the strong Protestant expansionism of the British Empire in the 1730s and a past perception of imperial glory revealed itself in a longing for the reign of Elizabeth through "pamphlets . . . drama, painting, poetry, and statuary."[29] In spite of, or perhaps because of, the political dimensions of this newfound taste, a heightened demand for Spenser's writing was met in the marketplace with books and pictures based on those texts.[30] During this period, Spenser was dubbed the Prince of English poets by publishers who reissued his work, and his epic became a staple of British gentlemen's education.[31]

No fewer than four new editions of *The Faerie Queene* appeared in England in 1715, 1751, 1758, and 1778. Additionally, the first exhaustive interpretative treatment of the poem, Thomas Warton's *Observations on the Fairy Queen of Spenser,* was printed in London in 1754 and reprinted in 1762, 1807, and 1820.[32] These mid-eighteenth-century interpretations tended to promote a romantic reading of the poem, with special privilege given to its Gothic and medievalizing sensibilities. Warton expressed the perceptions of his time:

> It was [Spenser's] business to engage the fancy, and to interest the attention by bold and striking images. . . . The various and the marvelous were the chief sources of delight. Hence we find our author ransacking alike the regions of reality and romance, of truth and fiction, to find the proper decorations and furniture of his fairy structure.[33]

West's introduction to the poet through this recently established critical vocabulary of romantic variety, global marvels, and ransacking adventures dovetailed with the artist's "exotic" North American background and his emerging taste for sublime imagery. Just as he had reshaped neoclassicism through his reformulation of history painting in *Wolfe,* West was prompted by *The Faerie Queene* to engage romantic aesthetic discourse.

New printings of *The Faerie Queene* drew the attention of artists, and West may well have consulted Thomas Birch's 1751 three-volume quarto edition featuring William Kent's thirty-two illustrations (figs. 11–13) interspersed throughout Spenser's verse.[34] Earlier English versions of *The Faerie Queene* were illustrated as well, but mostly by stock heraldic woodcuts used to divide the cantos and books. Kent's work was systematic and drew more or less directly on descriptions in the text itself. His illustrations represented the most elaborate and accessible earlier interpretation of Spenser. Like West, Kent concentrated his pictorial efforts on book 1—with almost half of the representations devoted to that book.[35] The illustrations were judged harshly, however. Horace Walpole decried Kent's images, though he owned a copy of the volume,[36] insisting that "whoever would search for his faults will find an ample crop in a very favourite work of his, the prints for Spenser's *Faerie Queene.*" Walpole continued his scathing appraisal of the illustrations' faults: "There are figures issuing from houses

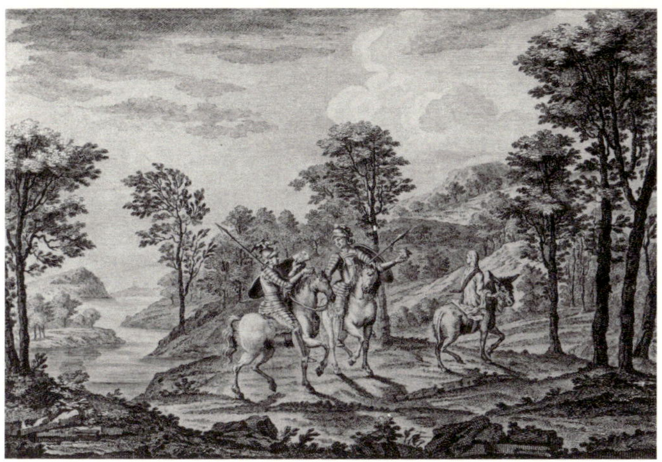

FIG. 11. William Kent, *Prince Arthur, the Redcross Knight, and Una,* in Edmund Spenser, *The Faerie Queene* (London, 1751)

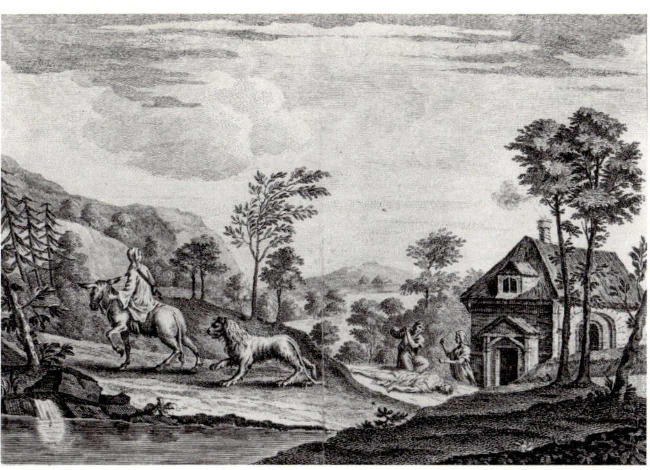

FIG. 12. William Kent, *Una's Escape from the Old Woman's House with her Lyon, after his Killing Kirkrapine,* in Edmund Spenser, *The Faerie Queene* (London, 1751)

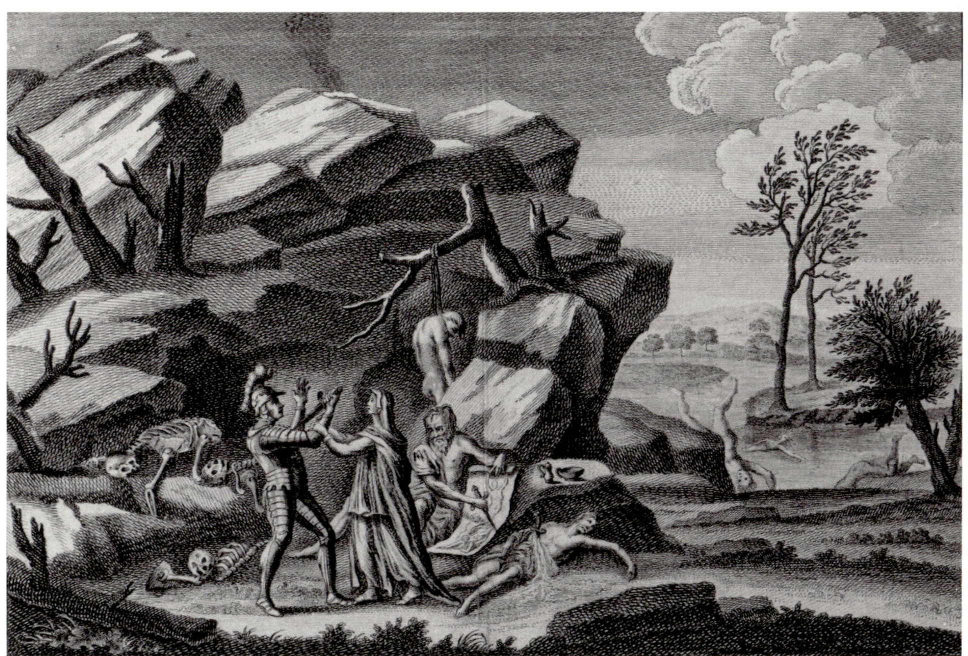

FIG. 13. William Kent, *The Redcross Knight over ruled by Dispair but timely saved by Una,* in Edmund Spenser, *The Faerie Queene* (London, 1751)

not so high as their shoulders, castles in which the towers could not contain an infant, and knights who hold their spears as men lifting a load sideways. The landscapes are the only tolerable parts."[37] Kent's illustrations did not provide West with direct models but introduced him to some of the poem's possibilities.

In looking to *The Faerie Queene*, West responded to a specific challenge issued by Joseph Warton, in 1764, for British artists to "search more frequently for subjects in the annals of England [as opposed to] Grecian or Roman stories."[38] At this time, Spenser was labeled as the "pictorial poet" par excellence, and *The Faerie Queene,* in particular, was "taken to be the quintessence of poetic pictorialism, a vivid and extensive exemplification of *ut pictura poesis*."[39] More than 175 depictions of the epic poem made in England attest to the widely held perception of the work's suitability for image making.[40] Subsequent artists based works on the epic, often turning to it as a source for character-inspired portraiture, as in Reynolds's *Miss Elizabeth Beauclerc as Una with the Lion* (fig. 14) and George Stubbs's elegant portrait of Isabella Saltonstall in his *Una and the Lion* (fig. 15). None of these works—except for a small watercolor by Swiss painter Henry Fuseli—were made earlier than West's.

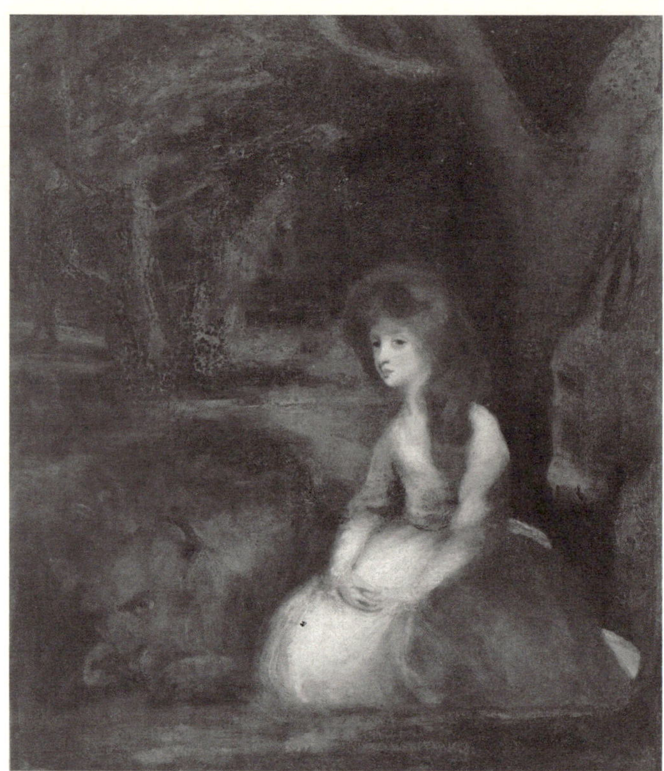

FIG. 14. Joshua Reynolds, *Miss Elizabeth Beauclerc as Una with the Lion,* 1777

Oil on canvas. Courtesy of the Fogg Art Museum, Harvard University Art Museums, Gift of Herbert Daniel Stone, 1963.1

West produced three major paintings in oil based on *The Faerie Queene* as well as numerous preparatory sketches. Each of the finished pictures was shown at the Royal Academy shortly after its completion. The artist painted copies of all three paintings in both oil and watercolor, and he took the additional step of having the works reproduced in copper line engravings or mezzotints for mass distribution. This body of work suggests the importance of the project for the artist, and each work individually represents West's complex stakes in a poem based on allegory and allegiance.

Spenser's text revolves around the Faerie Queene—known literally as Gloriana, or, allegorically, as Elizabeth—and her perfectly virtuous reign over a necessarily imperfect kingdom. West painted his way sequentially through the Christian epic, starting with book 1, which recounts the pursuit of holinesss. The principal characters in the narrative's initial section are Una and the Redcrosse Knight; one or both of these characters appear in each of West's finished compositions. As protagonists, they are also veiled personifications of truth and heroic devotion, twin qualities that are tested repeatedly throughout the course of the first book. In effect, Una and Redcrosse model lessons related to Christian belief and its chivalric expression for the reader. The narrative unfolds episodically through accounts of trial and error—quite literally in the encounter between Redcrosse and a monstrous serpent known as Errour in the first canto—building to a climax in which the knight and his female companion conquer evil and glimpse the goal of holiness in a landscape, only to have the knight turn away from that destination out of duty to serve his regent. The specific episodes that West chose to depict held complicated personal significance.

The first picture in West's series is *Una and the Lion* (cat. 2). The episode comes from early in book 1, canto 3, and through it Spenser allegorically promoted the power of truth over brute force. Una rests alone with her donkey in a wooded area, unaware of any danger, when a hungry lion approaches through the trees. Her purity and beauty save her from being devoured by the savage beast. West represents what might otherwise be handled in dramatic terms as a sober, idealized tableau. The modest, classically garbed female form of Una forms a stable and central focus for the horizontal composition. The emblematic beasts flank her, but they visually recede into the pastoral background as if to emphasize their secondary nature. As Helmut von Erffa and Allen Staley point out in their catalogue raisonné of West's work, the artist prepared several studies for the painting in ink and in chalk, focusing primarily on the pose and expression of the figure of Una (cats. 3, 4).[41]

When the painting was ready to be shown to the public, in 1771, the subject was still "sufficiently unfamiliar among art audiences that it required a full quotation of the relevant lines from *The Faerie Queene*."[42] The writer from the *Middlesex Journal* quoted stanzas three through six from the relevant canto:

> One day nigh wearie of the yrkesome way,
> From her vnhastie beast she did alight,
> And on the grasse her daintie limbes did lay
> In secret shadow, farre from all mens sight:
> From her faire head her fillet she vndight,
> And laid her stole aside. Her angels face
> As the great eye of heauen shyned bright,
> And made a sunshine in the shadie place;
> Did neuer mortall eye behold such heauenlt grace.

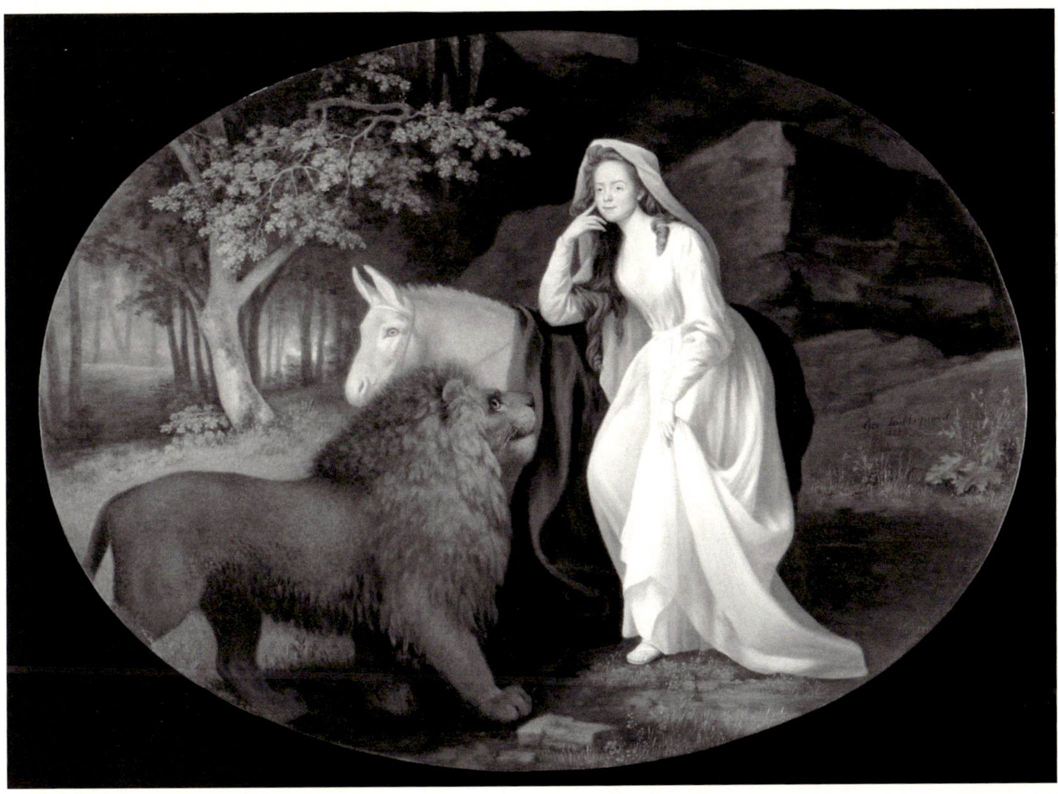

FIG. 15. George Stubbs, *Una and the Lion (Isabella Saltonstall as Una in Spenser's "Faerie Queene")*, 1782
Enamel on ceramic plaque. Fitzwilliam Museum, University of Cambridge, UK / Bridgeman Art Library

It fortuned out of the thickest wood
A ramping Lyon rushed suddainly,
Hunting full greedie after saluage blood;
Soone as the royalle virgin he did spy,
With gaping mouth at her ran greedily,
To haue at once deuour'd her tender corse:
But to pray when as he drew more ny,
His bloudie rage aswaged with remorse,
And with the sight amazd, forgat his furious forse.

In stead thereof he kist her wearie feet,
And lickt her lilly hands with fawny tong[43]

This citation does not include what likely concerned West. The sixth stanza was undoubtedly relevant to him as well.

As he her wronged innocence did weet,
O how can beautie maister the most strong,
And simple truth subdue auenging wrong?
Whose yeelded pride and proud submission,
Still dreading death, when she had marked long,
Her hart gan melt in great compassion,
And drizling tears did shed for pure affection.

The meaning of the passage turns on the paired questions posed in the middle of the last stanza: "How can beauty master the most strong, and [how can] simple truth subdue avenging wrong?" West might have asked a harsher set of questions examining current policies and suggesting more compassionate responses to rising conflicts in the colonies, even while offering a superficially flattering demonstration of filial piety to his primary patron, George III. Using this still somewhat unfamiliar literary subject, West could introduce subtle allegorical meanings that would otherwise trouble a public acquainted with his sources.

In 1770, when he would likely have begun the painting, the North American–born artist had good reasons to think in political as well as poetic terms about subjects that posited people of power acting in a merciful way when confronted by a beautiful and unspoiled truth in an Edenic landscape. Fellow colonists were growing increasingly intolerant of new taxes being unfairly levied on them as British subjects. They were even more outraged by the mounting tensions caused by British military occupation—best exemplified by the Boston Massacre in March 1770 during which five colonists were killed. West must have felt he could accomplish something meaningful through a work that suggested the transformation of hostilities into more reciprocal and stable balance of the weak and the strong. Allegory provided him with a means to show that admiration for beautiful principles might provide a way out for the British forces. In 1772, the year that West became historical painter to the king, he was represented at the second Royal Academy exhibition by this work.

At its first exhibition, *Una and the Lion* received little positive response. Horace Walpole dubbed it "a poor picture," criticized the length of Una's right leg as "ill drawn," and found no "dignity in the lion." The last comment was undoubtedly stinging since West may have intended the lion as a symbol of British royal might and was trying avidly to curry the monarch's favor. The historical moment into which the picture was introduced had some bearing on its reception. A decade later, when the work was shown for a second time at the Royal Academy, critical opinion had reversed: "The character of Una, by the President, is a design of such real merit, and greatness of style that I think I am warranted in saying he has made Virtue more lovely by it, and has shown us the human face divine."[44] The change owed a great deal to the artist's new status as president of the academy. Calling out "virtue" as a critical term demonstrated a familiarity with Spenser, something new to British art discourse. This later response testifies to West's accomplishment as allegorist. With *Una,* the American-born Royal Academician pleased the nationalistic English audience.

During West's rise to a position of high prestige within the late-eighteenth-century art world, other information about *Una and the Lion* came to light. A print after the work was published by John Boydell on August 10, 1772 (cat. 5). That engraving, by Richard Earlom, bears an inscription identifying Una as a known figure—Miss Mary Hall, born twenty-two years before in Jamaica. That the presumed sitter was, like West, a New World colonial

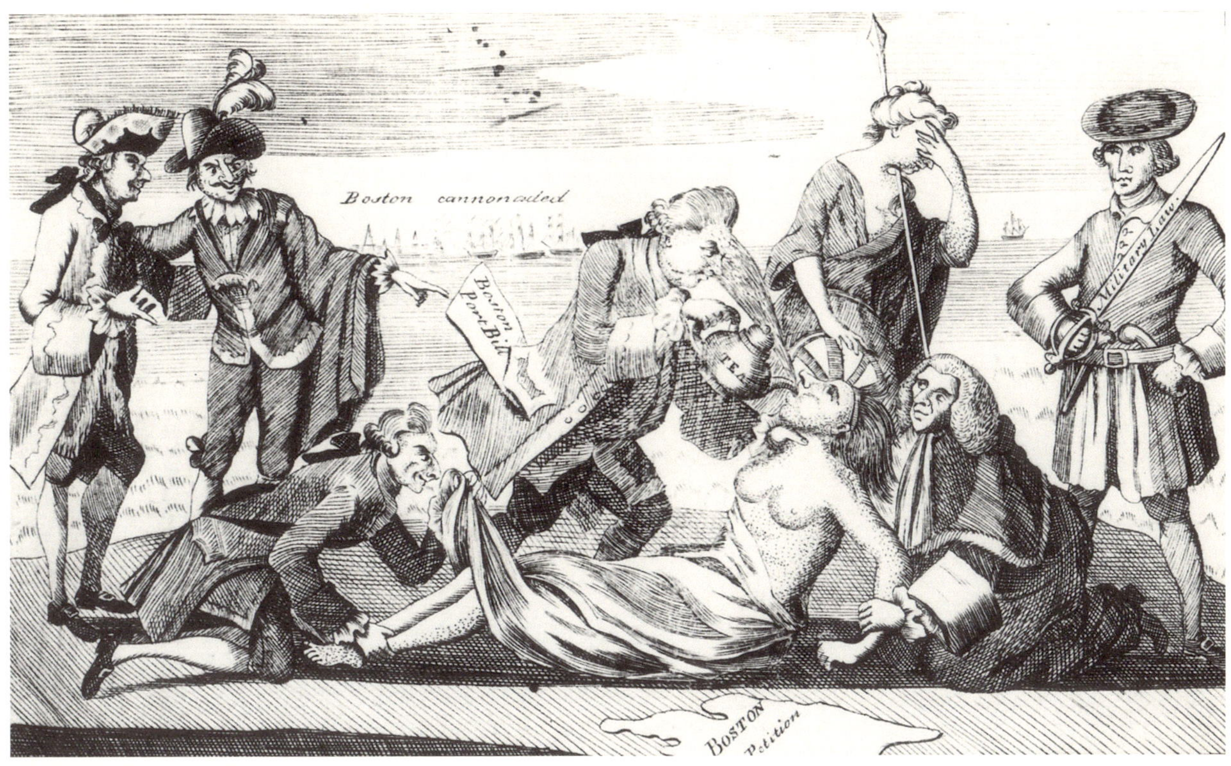

FIG. 16. Paul Revere, *The able Doctor, or America Swallowing the Bitter Draught,* 1774
Courtesy, American Antiquarian Society, Worcester, Massachusetts

subject, is revealing.[45] He may have chosen the framing narrative and her pose with this in mind. Reclining female figures in wooded landscapes would become, in the early nineteenth century, a well-known trope for a pure, but vulnerable America. Already in the late 1700s the subject had a certain allegorical legibility. Paul Revere used the concept of America as a besieged female figure in a 1774 political broadside in which representatives of British rule show no mercy toward the colonists and bear captions that identify them as proponents of "military law" and the "Boston port bill" (fig. 16).[46] By now, the incommensurable disagreements between the British Empire and its colonial subjects had been stretched to the limit and would shortly resolve themselves in outright calls for independence. Allegory proved helpful in responding to this situation, and West's next work, *The Cave of Despair,* confirms the flexibility of allegory as a device.

While *Una and the Lion* was still on display in London, West was probably at work on his second Spenserian subject, based on a much later section of book 1 (cat. 7). The allegory turns to the crisis of lost faith that affects even the most faithful. The painting is dark in both mood and color. Gray shadows surround a central figural group whose actions spiral from the outstretched hands of Una and the knife-wielding arms of her traveling companion, Redcrosse. Sitting passively is a sinister personification of Despair—a disheveled old man who inspires the waves of self-destruction surrounding him. According to canto 9, the Christian knight is drawn to the cave to avenge the death of fellow knight Trevisan, but instead is convinced by Despair to take his own life. Truth prevents Christian virtue from completing this desperate act. The work is different from West's first Spenserian subject in both its formal handling and its essential grim tone. It is visually dark and compositionally detailed. Proof of the work's close temporal and didactic rapport with *Una and the Lion* is seen in the reuse of a preparatory drawing for the donkey's head (cat. 8).

Although physically smaller than the other *Faerie Queene* paintings, *The Cave of Despair* ultimately became the best known of West's three Spenserian subjects.[47] The picture was identified in the artist's time as one of the most sublime sections of *The Fairie Queene*.[48] Like *Una and the Lion*, *The Cave of Despair* inspired British romantic artists for subsequent generations. West conceivably encountered the narrative first through Kent's illustration in the 1751 edition of Spenser's text, and he possibly knew Fuseli's watercolor done just a few years before.

What is critical to note is how West's interpretation differs from these precedents. West has collapsed several independent moments from the narrative. The first comes from near the middle of the canto:

> That darksome cave they enter, where they find
> That cursed man, low sitting on the ground,
> Musing full sadly in his sullein mind;
> His griesie lockes, long growen, and unbound,
> Disorderd hong about his shoulders round,
> And hid his face; through which his hollow eyne
> Lookt deadly dull, and stared as astound;
> His raw-bone cheeks through penurie and pine,
> Were shronke into his iawes, as he did neuer dine.
>
> His garment nought but many ragged clouts.
> With thornes together pins and patched was,
> The which his naked sides he wrapt abouts;
> And him beside there lay vpon the gras,
> A drearie corse whose life away dis pas,
> All wallowd in his owne yet luke-warme blood,
> That from a wound yet welled fresh alas;
> In which a rustie knife fast fixed stood,
> And made an open passage for the gushing flood.
>
> (bk. 1, canto 9, xxxv–xxxvi)

The second section appears as the penultimate verses in the canto, in which the ostensible hero, the Redcrosse Knight, gives up all hope:

> But when as none of them he saw him take,
> He to him raught a dagger sharpe and keene,
> And gaue it him in hand: his hand did quake,
> And tremble like a leafe of Aspin greene,
> And troubled bloud through his pale face was seene
> To come, and goe with tidings from the hart,
> As it a running messenger had beene.
> At last resolu'd to worke his finall smart,
> He lifted vp his hande, and backe againe did start.
>
> Which when as *Vna* heard, through euery vaine,
> The crudled cold ran to her well of life,
> As in a swone: but soone reliu'd againe,
> Out of his hand she snatcht the cursed knife,
> Amd threw it to the ground, enraged rife,
> And to him said, Fie fie, faint harted knight,
> What meanest thou by this repochfull strife?
> Is this the battell which thou vuanst to fight
> With that fire-mouthed Dragon, horrible and bright?
>
> (bk. 1, canto 9, li–lii)

West combined a moment of accumulated description with a moment of tense action—the very instant in which Una reaches out to arrest the hand of Redcrosse. Despair looks on without registering any discernible reaction. The general solemnity and shadowy silhouettes suggest, but do not reveal, the moment's ultimate dramatic importance. Preparatory drawings show other elements of the composition worked out with great clarity (cats. 9, 10). The thrust of *The Cave of Despair* episode shows how easily heroic self-confidence is undone by un-Christian impulses. Despair, a satanic force, will repeatedly wipe out virtue without a second thought. Redcrosse has unwisely abandoned reason and higher purpose—"How will you battle the dragon you so want to fight?" the figure of Truth demands as she intervenes decisively in the drama. West was worrying about righteous battles to come.

As West appropriated them, the characters in *The Cave of Despair* have multiple identities. Redcrosse embodies several distinctly symbolic selves—he is deliberately and at once Redcrosse, the chivalrous defender of Queene

Gloriana and Una, and St. George, who perceives his true identity and defeats a dragon in the final canto of book 1. For West, Redcrosse represented the figure of King George III as well. The crested armor, the shared name, and the role as chief protagonist promote such an identification. Read this way, the episode in which Una/Truth/America tries to stop Redcrosse/St. George/King George from doing away with himself might seem paradoxical. However, as an expression of West's increasing sense of personal conflict, the episode begins to take on a meaningful shape. The artist undoubtedly struggled with the colonies' rising discontentment with England while seeking to demonstrate an unfailing allegiance to his patron. Spenser's allegory provided a backdrop against which both the political exigencies brought on by revolution and a desire for merciful intervention could be safely expressed.

The Cave of Despair struck a resonant chord with sectors of the British public. Notwithstanding Walpole's sweeping dismissal of the work, West's painting has been held up as a proto-romantic masterpiece because of its dark mood and sublime violence. The image was engraved by Henry Moses in 1811 for a celebratory publication of West's greatest works, and one of the greatest painters in British art history, Joseph Mallord William Turner, wished he had purchased the painting when it was sold at auction after the artist's death.[49] As several scholars have speculated, West may have drawn on Edmund Burke's *A Philosophical Enquiry into the Origins of Our Ideas of the Sublime and Beautiful* (1757) while he was consulting Spenser when making the painting.[50] West's most recent biographer has shown that the artist was personally introduced to Thomas Paine by Burke in the 1780s, which was likely recorded against him as proof of his silently held antagonism toward the monarchy.[51] West probably shared Burke's outspoken sympathy for the American struggle for independence as conveyed in Burke's speeches to the British House of Commons and other published writings of the time.[52]

West's wish to stop supremely self-destructive acts—a military or monarchy in danger of destroying itself in its punition of subjects abroad—was a historically potent statement. It was also impossible to formulate and could perhaps only be proposed symbolically or allegorically. West practiced this in other works of the time, as when he depicted the king's radiant recovery from bouts of a recurring mental illness, now known to be the disease porphyria. For scholars, the distinguishing feature of *The Cave of Despair* was that it signaled a decisive change in the artist's painting practice: he was no longer interested in a strictly neoclassical aesthetic stance, characterized by didactic meanings and legibility of expression. This was not the only contribution that *The Faerie Queene* suggested for West. The final example from his Spenserian excursion steps back slightly from that formally extreme and self-destructive position, just as the narrative of *The Faerie Queene* vacillates between excess and final triumph at the close of book 1.

The Timken Museum of Art's *Fidelia and Speranza* (cat. 1) was West's last easel picture in the series. In many ways, it is the most complicated and competent demonstration of his broadening interest in allegorical painting. The work was executed in 1776, a significant year in the chronology of the American Revolution. Perhaps for this reason, the painting bears a deliberately legible signature and date. It hardly matters whether the painting was started before or after July 4. By this time, West was unquestionably aware of movements in Philadelphia to organize the First Continental Congress and to forcibly resist British occupation and taxation, and he would have certainly known about the military fire exchanged at Lexington, Massachusetts. The painting's narrative can be read with these episodes in mind, albeit in only allegorical terms.

The text, from canto 10, describes what happens immediately after the Cave of Despair episode. Una leads a distraught and spiritually broken Redcrosse knight to the House of Holiness for rehabilitation. He and Una emerge from the left middle ground of the composition, riding out of a cloud-darkened landscape. The pictorial source for these diminutive figures on horseback might have come directly from Kent's engravings or from other engraved works of the period.[53] The overall emphasis is on the two contrasting female figures standing near the center of the canvas. These principal actors in the selected scene are described in the poem:

Thus as they gan of sundry things deuise,
Loe two most goodly virgins came in place,
Ylinked arme in arme in louely wise,
With countenance demure and modest grace,
They numbred euen steps and equall pace;
Of which the eldest that *Fidelia* hight;
Like sunny beames threw from her christall face,
That coud haue dazd the rash beholders sight
And round about her head did shine like heauens light.

She was araied all in lilly white,
And in her right hand bore a cup of gold,
With wine and water fild vp to the hight,
In which a Serpent did himselfe engfold,
That horrour made to all, that did behold;
But she no whit did chaunge her constant mood;
And in her other hand she fast did hold
A booke, that was signed and seald with blood,
Wherin darke things were writ, hard to be vnderstood.

Her younger sister, that *Speranza* hight,
Was clad in blew, that her beseemed well;
Not all so cheerful seemed she of sight,
As was her sister; whether dread did well,
Or anguish in her hart, is hard to tell:

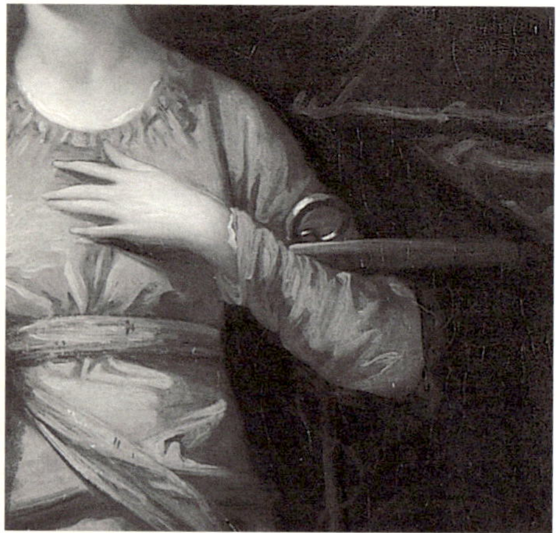

FIG. 17. Benjamin West, detail of anchor, cat. 1

Upon her arm a siluer anchor lay,
Whereon she leaned euer, as befell;
And euer vp to heaven, as she did pray,
Her steadfast eyes were bent, ne swarued other way.

(bk. 1, canto 10, xii–xiv)

A comparison of verse and painting shows the remarkable degree to which West was faithful to his source. Faith and Hope, cardinal virtues, are given center stage. The emblematic details recounted in Spenser's verse—Hope's anchor (fig. 17), Faith's firm possession of the New Testament and grail-like chalice, and the directionality of their gazes—are depicted in the finished picture.[54] West also produced an ink drawing of *Charity* (Charissa), another figure who appears in this section of the text, but that work may not be strictly related to this project (fig. 18). What West invents, however, is more interesting than what he carefully adheres to in his close reading of Spenser. From the rather innocuous cue that the two women advance "linked arm in arm," the artist suggests a masterfully intertwined sensibility that pervades the entire work.[55] This is expressed in multiple levels in the composition and, potentially, in its interpretation.

To begin, West ensured an irrefutable link to his earlier Spenserian compositions by reusing, for a third time, the sketch of a donkey head in his treatment of Una's mount. The vines hanging above the arched doorway are twisted together just as the arms of Fidelia and Speranza are gracefully intertwined. In the same way, the classicizing costumes worn by the women are not merely draped over their long bodies but are elaborately wrapped and, in the case of Speranza, bind the torso with what appears to be an almost painful force. The hairstyles similarly demonstrate an extravagantly animated, almost obsessively braided invention. A snake emerges from Speranza's golden chalice in a serpentine echo of this underlying convolution. Even the rose-colored pentimenti visible beneath the fingers of the women betray a spreading and contracting action that heightens the overall pattern of tense, interdependent exchanges.

If Una's leading of Redcrosse is emblematic of a mentally worn and physically injured monarchy, Fidelia and

Speranza are his prescriptive balms. The balance and harmonious contrast that initially seem to pervade the painting are subverted by a sense of entanglement that matches West's mixed state of mind. Allegorically, George (both St. George and King George) can only be restored from the increasingly miserable plight in the closing cantos of book 1 (and in 1776) through the intercession of such Christian virtues as Faith and Hope. In the year of his countrymen's Declaration of Independence, West wished, as Spenser might have before him, for a safe means of expressing his will toward independence, free of the confines of desperate control. Such a desire was overcome, however, by West's greater concern for his continued prosperity and successful career.

By contrast, when John Singleton Copley painted the identical scene from *The Faerie Queene* almost twenty years after West, he evidenced none of the ambivalence that West registers in his composition (fig. 19). Copley took *Fidelia and Speranza* as an opportunity to paint his three children—John in the role of Redcrosse and daughters Elizabeth and Mary as Fidelia and Speranza—inscribing them, as well as himself, into what had become a successful mainstay of literary portraiture. Copley's Redcrosse, like the elder artist himself, expresses confidence as he struts into a luminous space as the female actors respond demurely to his entrance. Copley's accommodation to life in Britain, after leaving Boston in 1774, was uncomplicated by regret or venal obligations. For him, Spenser represented an opportunity to engage in a dialogue with other artists of his time, perhaps no one more than his countryman West, and he sought to outdo West in terms of scale and optimism.

Other works that Benjamin West produced around the time he was completing *The Faerie Queene* sequence deserve discussion. In 1776 the artist was preoccupied with a series of portrait commissions for the royal family, including separate portrayals of the king, the king and queen together, and their six children as a group, and a double portrait of the queen and her daughter (fig. 20). The double portrait is similar in organization to *Fidelia and Speranza*, although it is presented in a horizontal, not vertical, format. Interestingly, it features Queen Charlotte and the Princess Royal,

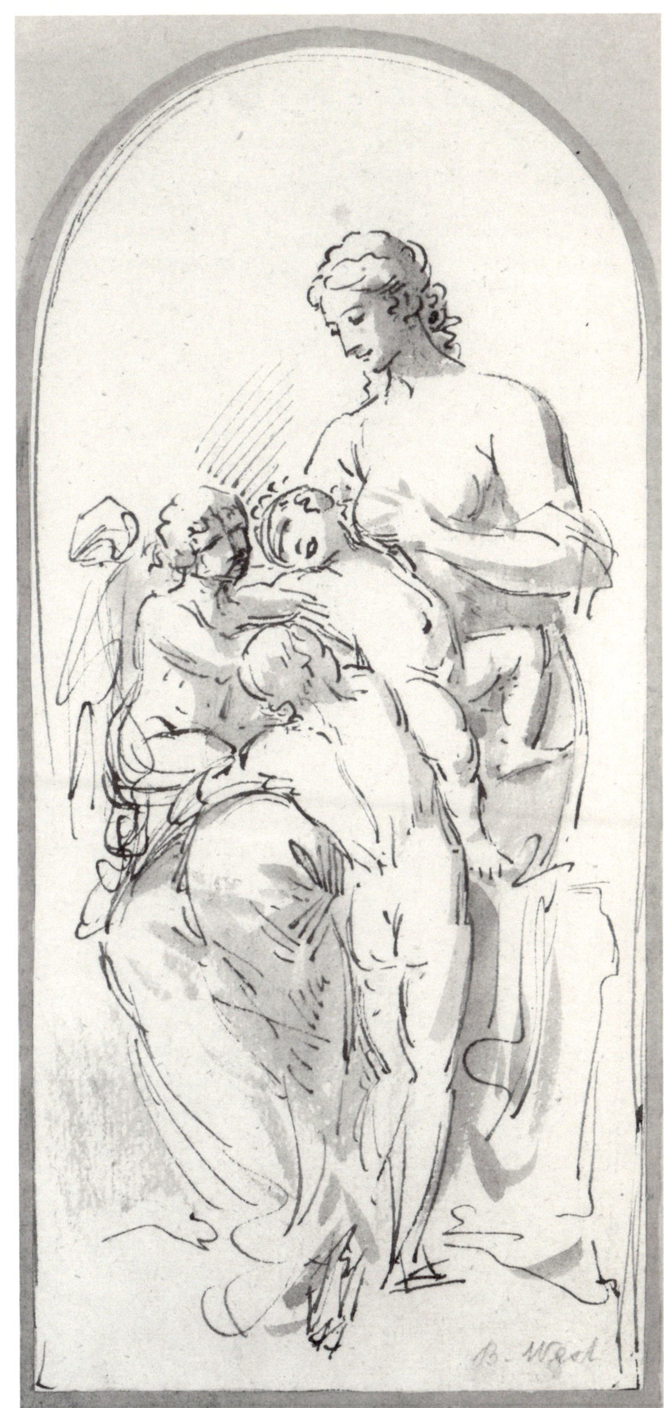

FIG. 18. Benjamin West, *Charity*

Drawing. National Gallery of Art, Washington, Gift of Robert S. Pirie, 1981.77.4.(DR)

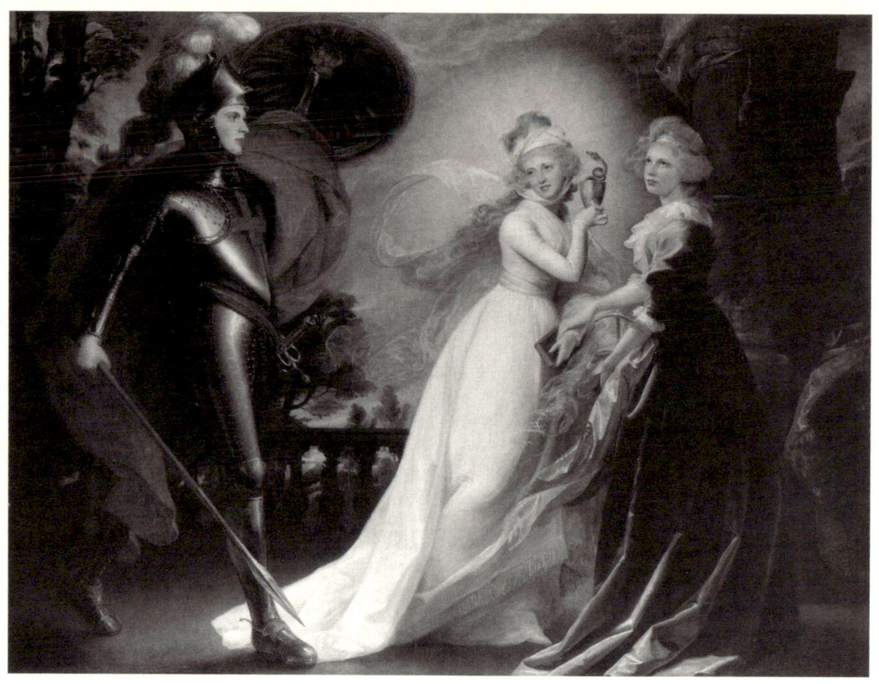

FIG. 19. John Singleton Copley, *The Red Cross Knight,* 1793

Oil on canvas. National Gallery of Art, Washington, Gift of Mrs. Gordon Dexter, 1942.4.2.551(PA)

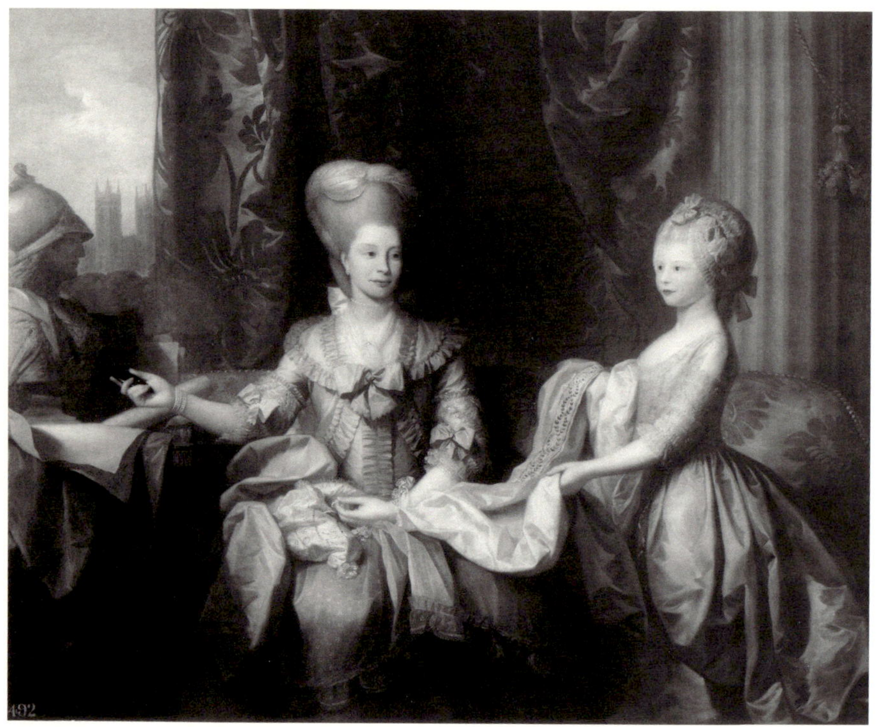

FIG. 20. Benjamin West, *Queen Charlotte with Charlotte, Princess Royal,* 1776

Oil on canvas. The Royal Collection © HM Queen Elizabeth II

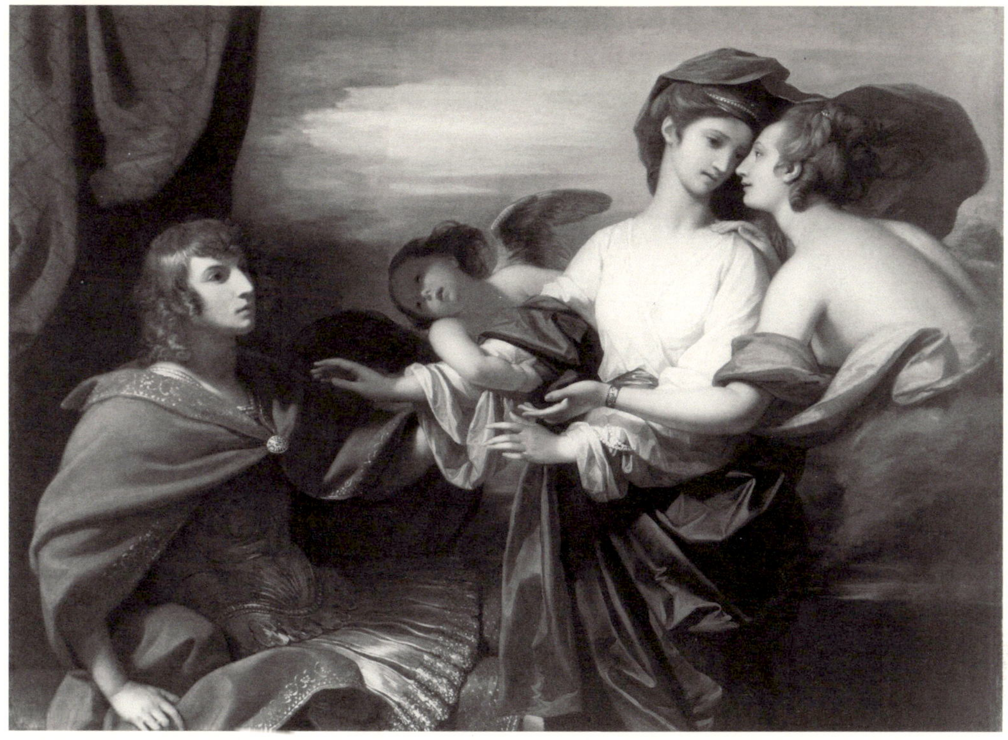

FIG. 21. Benjamin West, *Helen Brought to Paris,* 1776
Oil on canvas. Smithsonian American Art Museum, Museum purchase, 1969.33

Charlotte, working at needlepoint. They are joined by the activity of weaving together strands to create an image, just as West had been allegorically threading personal and political strands in the Spenserian subjects. Another portrait draws even more conspicuously on the structure seen in *Fidelia and Speranza*. West's large-scale depiction of *Mrs. Jean Dundas and Her Daughter, Grizell* (1777, private collection) shows the two women in basically comparable poses to the virtuous figures in the Timken work. Details such as hairstyle, costume, and elongation of bodies further signal shared pictorial strategies.[56]

Addressing another epic subject, West produced a major picture—almost as large as Una and slightly bigger than *Fidelia and Speranza*—that drew from the *Iliad: Helen Brought to Paris* (fig. 21). Combining devices learned throughout the *Faerie Queene* project, the work displays a similarly strong interest in intertwined bodies, with a dense network of arms, fabrics, and exchanged gazes directing the viewer both toward and away from the tangled pictorial center.

Of all the contemporaneous works, perhaps the most suggestive comparison in its potential relationship to the *Faerie Queene* narratives may be the life-size twin portrait of Colonel Guy Johnson and Karonghyontye (fig. 22). West may have made this portrait while at work on *Fidelia and Speranza*. If this is the case, a number of striking parallels emerge.[57] The work purportedly shows Guy Johnson, the colonial superintendent of Indian affairs, seated with a Native American behind him—tentatively identified as Karonghyontye, a Mohawk subaltern within the British military forces occupying North America. If the dating of this work is correct, West returned once more to the symbolic space of *The Death of General Wolfe* some five years after its debut. Whether he was coyly reminding the public of his earlier successes with his native subjects or trying to layer his current historical portraits with a charged contem-

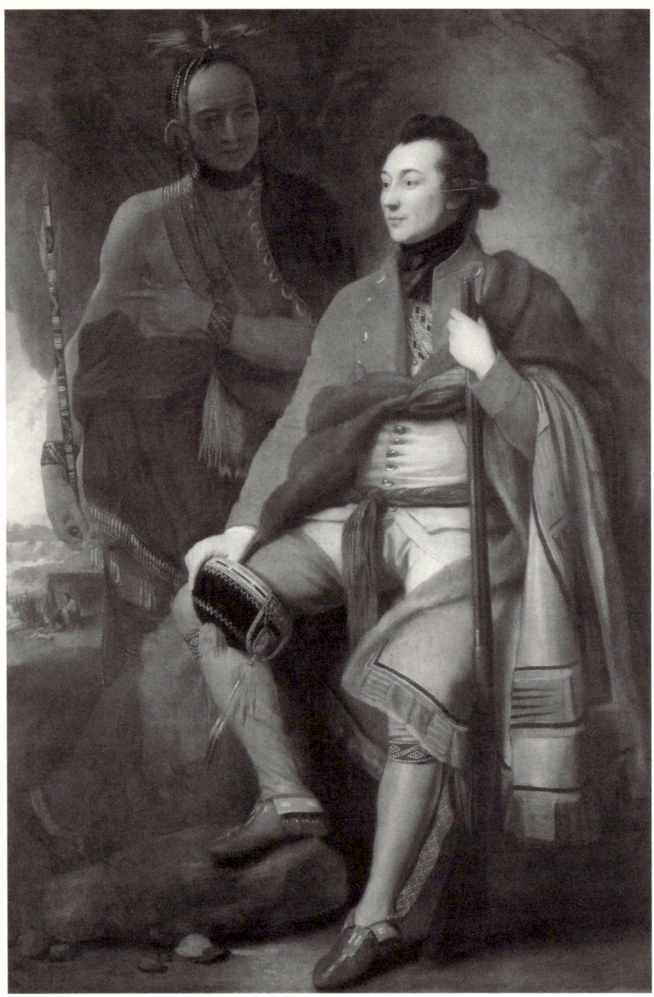

FIG. 22. Benjamin West, *Colonel Guy Johnson and Karonghyontye (Captain David Hill),* 1776

Oil on canvas. National Gallery of Art, Washington, Andrew W. Mellon Collection, 1940.1.10.(PA)

porary relevance is pure speculation. Regardless, the fundamental composition of the image bears an affinity with West's last Spenserian treatment: two figures, placed to the right of center of a cavelike composition, with a diminutive figural group rendered in precisely the same proportion and level within the middle distance to the left. The conspicuously presented peace pipe in Karonghyontye's left hand and the intricacy with which the artist has wrapped Johnson's overgarment and belt are reminiscent of similar motifs in *Fidelia and Speranza*. It is impossible to know for certain if West wanted to insist on the connection, but the painting stands out as his last great effort to make plain his attachment to North America, his native soil, at the height of the Revolution.

The predicament in which West at once thrived as an artist, struggled as a colonial subject, and sought virtuous resolution through an investigation of *The Faerie Queene* could be dismissed as a purely rhetorical construct. William Empson warned about such ambiguity when he recognized that inquiries into Elizabethan allegory of the kind Spenser created can yield a "variety of meanings [that have] been blurred into generalization and you can read all kinds of political interpretations, indeed any interpretations that come naturally to you, into a story offered as interesting in itself."[58] Yet this is not what is at stake in any speculative reading of West's allegorical intentions. His work begs to be understood in more complex terms than has become customary. In an important contribution to West scholarship, Helmut von Erffa questioned the hidden logic at work during the years that the artist emerged as a major figure in British painting and proposed that he might have been driven by a previously unremarked struggle with mortal themes:

> Why are the heroes always dying in his early paintings? . . . From the dying Wolfe . . . he goes to a less heroic fear of death, or closeness of death in the *Cave of Despair*, where the hero of Spenser's Faerie Queene, the *Red Cross Knight*, is surrounded by dispatched corpses "wallowing in blood." While he is saved by Una, the hapless Saul of the Old Testament [the reference here is to the nearly contemporaneous work *Saul and the Witch of Endor* (1777, Wadsworth Atheneum, Hartford, Conn.)] ends a suicide in battle.[59]

Could it be that a impending sense of dread infiltrated the artist's works of the 1770s as he worried about the emerging conflict between his conduct and his conscience? West connected to *The Faerie Queene* at a deep, personal level—he kept several of the Spenserian paintings with him until his death for this reason.

A vivid exchange between Spenser's imaginary Fairyland and West's conflicted attitudes toward imperial

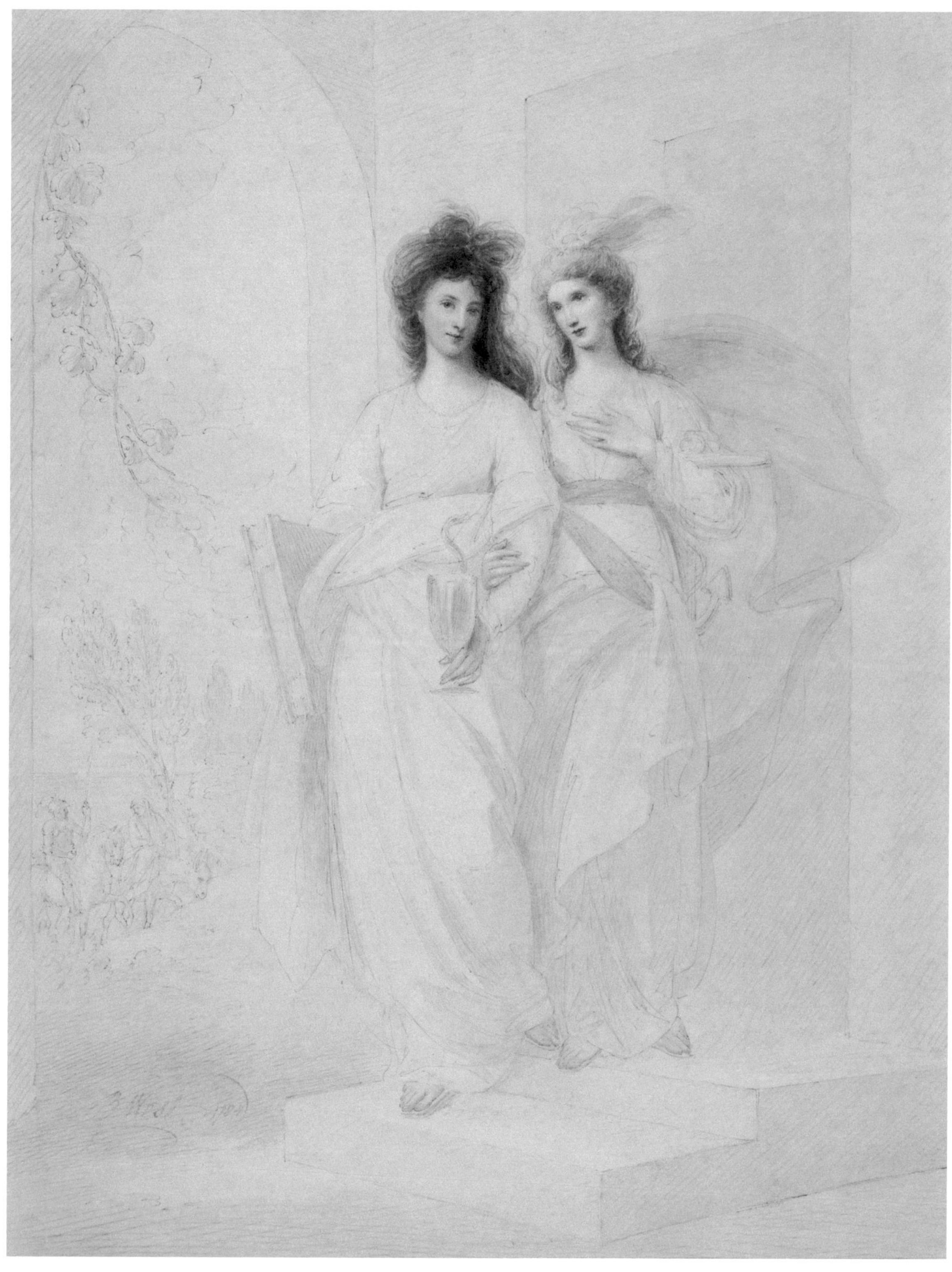

FIG. 23. Benjamin West, *Fidelia and Speranza,* 1784

Watercolor and brown ink on paper. Courtesy of the Fogg Art Museum, Harvard University Art Museums, Bequest of Grenville L. Winthrop. Photo: Katya Kallsen © 2004 President and Fellows of Harvard College

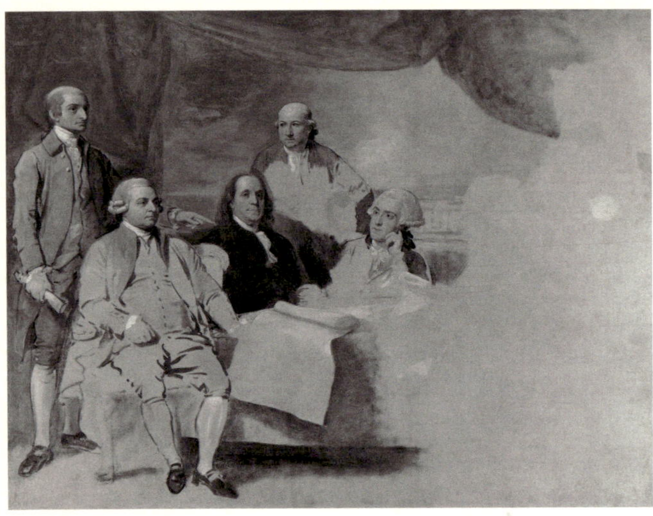

FIG. 24. Benjamin West, *The Signing of the Preliminary Treaty of Peace, 1782,* 1783
Oil on canvas. Courtesy, Winterthur Museum

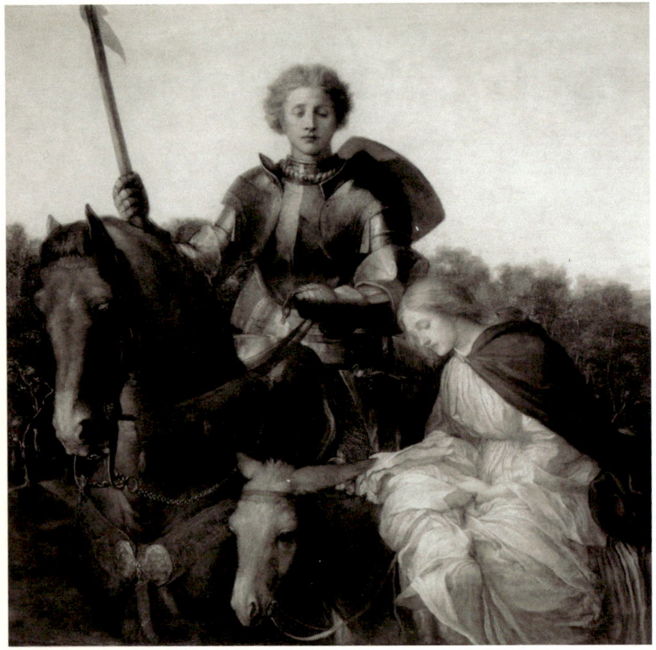

FIG. 25. George Frederick Watts, *Una and the Red Cross Knight,* 1869
Oil on canvas. Collection, Art Gallery of Western Australia

conquest of the New World exists and can be read through this entire series of works. West could have picked up the association on Spenser's dedication page where Elizabeth is identified as the "Queene of England, France, Ireland, and of Virginia" or in Spenser's text itself: "all that now America men call" (bk. 2, canto 10, lxxii). Scholars from the eighteenth century to the present have recognized that the allegorical layers of the epic can be peeled back to reveal an easy substitution of chivalric adventures in Fairyland for colonial exploits in North and Central America.[60] Interpreting West's pictorial investigations of Spenser with this literary critical insight suggests a new route for future scholarship on the most famous American-born artist working in eighteenth-century England.

West abandoned *The Faerie Queene* as a subject in 1784, when he executed a watercolor after *Fidelia and Speranza* (fig. 23). In this work Faith and Hope stand alone in a sheltered, protected space. The year before West made this final image, the British government recognized American independence at Versailles and ceded control of the North American lands to the former colonists. West's suggestively unfinished historical painting, *The Signing of the Preliminary Treaty of Peace, 1782* (fig. 24), conceivably took the artist away from the crossed allegiances that had nagged him since his arrival in London. The work shows West's close friend, Benjamin Franklin, and other signatories of a truce with England, in another contemporary historical painting. The scene did not present West with an opportunity to allegorize a dignified way out for George III and, in this sense, is completely different from the *Faerie Queene* sequence. By this time West was otherwise preoccupied with a new series of royal commissions—a major decorative cycle interpreting British medieval glory and work for the king's chapel at Windsor Castle.[61]

The Faerie Queene inspired generations of artists after West, including many in the United States. *Una and the Lion* became a popular subject. American artists, such as Washington Allston, painted *Faerie Queene* subjects multiple times, and British Pre-Raphaelites took on the subject with renewed energy (fig. 25). Still, few painters treated the subject with the same charged sobriety as West. Walter

Crane's illustrations for George Allen's revised editions of the Spenser classic, published between 1894 and 1896, remain a landmark in the history of the book and may have been distantly inspired by West.[62] The most ostentatious effort to take on Spenser's epic can be found at the Enoch Pratt Free Library in Baltimore, Maryland, where Lee Woodward Zeigler covered two thousand square feet of wall surface with eighteen episodes from the six books (fig. 26). Zeigler worked on the monumental cycle for seven years. At the public unveiling on October 14, 1945, Elizabethan scholar Charles Grosvenor Osgood praised the representations and wished selfishly that Spenser was present to witness the enduring interest in his narrative. Osgood pointed out that Spenser's times were even more challenging than the difficult period through which the United States was then passing:

> The Faerie Queene is "escape" poetry but, like all great art, it is an escape from unreality to reality. And may we not hope that through this splendid pictured commentary many a person dissatisfied with the unreality of his life may find his way into a safer region of reality, whence he may bring back some measure of that transforming power which turns insignificance into significance?[63]

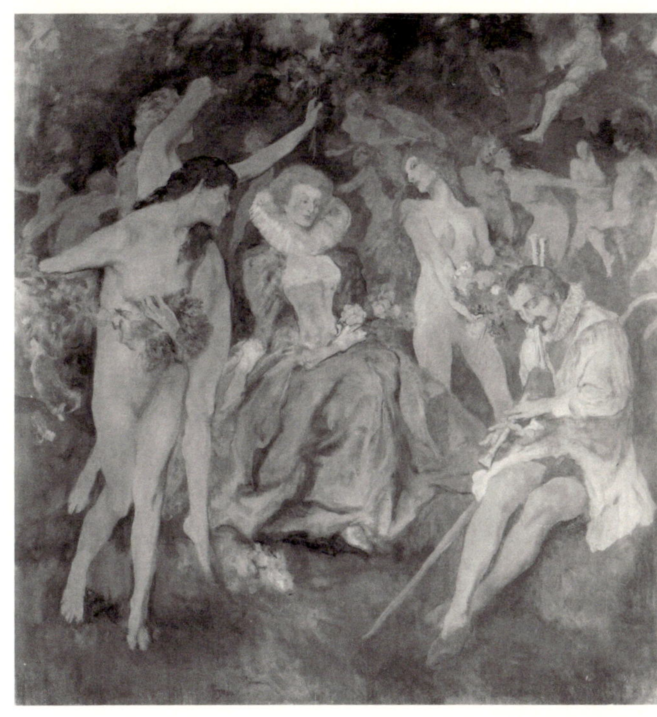

FIG. 26. Lee Woodward Zeigler, *The Faerie Queen Murals,* c. 1941
Enoch Pratt Free Library, Baltimore, Maryland

As Osgood notes, powerful works of art have the capacity to transform both their makers and their audiences. By using *The Faerie Queene*, West was doing more than just paying tribute to Spenser. He was disentangling himself from the many personal, political, and pictorial struggles that he faced in the 1770s. This effort led him not to "escape," to use Osgood's sentiment, but to create a productive exploration of the most heavily freighted allegorical narrative available at the time. In the end, West's interest encompassed the most profoundly successful period of his career, and his Spenserian subjects provided new sources for original aesthetic debates and an outlet for highly coded political critique.

NOTES

1. *The Departure of Regulus from Rome* (1769, Royal Collection) clinched West's reputation in London, having "met with virtually unanimous approval at the Royal Academy's inaugural exhibition." See David Solkin, *Painting for Money: The Visual Arts in the Public Sphere in Eighteenth-Century England* (New Haven: Yale University Press, 1993), p. 268.

2. West has enjoyed sustained attention from eminent scholars in American art. The appearance of certain names in these notes—Helmut von Erffa, Allen Staley, Jules Prown, Ann Uhry Abrams, Vivien Green Fryd, Susan Rather, in particular—demonstrates my admiration for their efforts. The monumental contribution of von Erffa and Staley, *The Paintings of Benjamin West* (New Haven: Yale University Press, 1986), merits special acknowledgment. Nonetheless, with the exception of other studies—notably Alexander Nemerov, "The Ashes of Germanicus and the Skin of Painting: Sublimation and Money in Benjamin West's *Agrippina*," *Yale Journal of Criticism* 11 (1998): 11–27, and Simon Schama, *Dead Certainties: Unwarranted Speculations* (New York: Alfred A. Knopf, 1991)—little has been done to suggest West's vitality as a source for new art history.

3. Nemerov describes the situation succinctly: "West's paintings have received only limited scholarly attention. . . . They have generally not received the kind of close analysis scholars bestow upon difficult, complicated works of art. The implicit understanding is that West's paintings, even if they contain an allegory or two, are fundamentally straightforward. Yet this understanding obscures some of the provocative tensions in West's art." See Nemerov, "The Ashes of Germanicus," p. 11.

4. Although West was not a practicing Quaker, his family background and public presumption often linked him to that religious sect, at least until he formally joined the Anglican Church in England around the time of his marriage. See Jules Prown, "Benjamin West and the Use of Antiquity," *American Art* 10 (Summer 1996): 35. Three children were from John West's first marriage to Elizabeth Beisley, who died in childbirth, and ten were from his second marriage, to Sarah Pearson. Robert C. Alberts, *Benjamin West: A Biography* (Boston: Houghton Mifflin Company, 1978), 12.

5. On Williams's oeuvre, see William H. Gerdts, "William Williams: New Discoveries," *Winterthur Portfolio* 4 (1968): 159–67, esp. 165–66; also see Susan Rather, "Benjamin West's Professional Endgame and the Historical Conundrum of William Williams," *William and Mary Quarterly* 59 (October 2002): 821–64.

6. The name Haidt also appears as Heidt in some texts. See Allen Staley's careful account of the West's early years, in *Benjamin West: American Painter at the English Court* (Baltimore: Baltimore Museum of Art, 1989), p. 14; also see Ann Uhry Abrams, "A New Light on Benjamin West's Pennsylvania Instruction," *Winterthur Portfolio* 17 (Winter 1982): 243–57.

7. See Jules David Prown, "Two Early Drawings by West," in *Art as Evidence: Writings on Art and Material Culture* (New Haven: Yale University Art Gallery, 2001), p. 115 n. 8.

8. Von Erffa and Staley point out that West did not strictly copy the engraving by Hubert Gravelot as it appeared appeared in Rollin's text, which appeared in English between 1738 and 1740; the eighteen-year-old elaborated and embellished the small source image in its translation to a large oil painting. See von Erffa and Staley, *The Paintings of Benjamin West*, pp. 10–11, 156.

9. John Galt, *The Life, Studies, and Works of Benjamin West, Esq. President of the Royal Academy of London, Composed from Materials furnished by Himself*, 2 vols. (London: T. Cadell, 1820), 1:104–6. Prown has pointed out that in naively pronouncing this resemblance, West played on shared ideas of the "noble savage" in vogue at the moment. See Prown, "Benjamin West and the Use of Antiquity."

10. For the summary of these Italian years, I have relied on a variety of sources. Most important, I have consulted the most recent and thorough biography of West by Alberts, *Benjamin West: A Biography*, pp. 41–50. *The World of Benjamin West* (Allentown, Pa.: Allentown Museum of Art, 1962) provides a more prosaic account of these travels (see pp. 21–25). See also Staley, *Benjamin West: American Painter at the English Court*, pp. 30–31; and Prown, "Benjamin West and the Use of Antiquity," pp. 30–34. All of these sources make use of John Galt's early biography, *The Life, Studies, and Works of Benjamin West, Esq.*, and all remark on its limitations as an authoritative source.

11. On Dryden's late-eighteenth-century popularity, see Ann Uhry Abrams, *The Valiant Hero: Benjamin West and Grand Style History Painting* (Washington, D.C.: Smithsonian Institution Press, 1985), p. 121.

12. The other great sixteenth-century precedent for Spenser's *Faerie Queene*, also in Italian, was Torquato Tasso's *Gerusalemme Liberata*, which provided West with the subject of *Rinaldo and Armida*, which he painted no fewer than five times between 1766 and 1797. See von Erffa and Staley, *The Paintings of Benjamin West*, pp. 282–84.

13. On West's relationship with Kauffmann, see Abrams, *The Valiant Hero*, pp. 82–87.

14. Ibid., pp. 107–8.

15. For a complete discussion of eighteenth-century British cultural tastes, see John Brewer, *The Pleasures of the Imagination: English Culture in the Eighteenth Century* (New York: Farrar, Straus and Giroux, 1997), esp. pp. 201–321.

16. In his "Letter to Ralegh," Spenser mentions both Ariosto and Tasso by name as favorites. See A. Bartlett Giamatti, *Play of the Double Senses: Spenser's Faerie Queene* (Englewood Cliffs, N.J.: Prentice-Hall, 1975), p. 11.

17. The first of these illustrations—*Savage Warrior Taking Leave of His Family*—was published in Venice in 1763 in *Storei degli stablimenti europei in America.* His former patron, William Smith, commissioned a pair of other works for *An Historical Account of the Expedition against the Ohio Indians* published in London in 1766. See Prown, "Two Early Drawings," for a full discussion of these commissions.

18. Prown, "Two Early Drawings," p. 112.

19. Reynolds, quoted in Charles Mitchell, "Benjamin West's 'Death of General Wolfe' and the Popular History Piece," *Journal of the Warburg and Courtauld Institutes* 7 (1944): 20.

20. West, quoted in Prown, "Benjamin West and the Use of Antiquity," p. 40.

21. Reynolds, quoted in Charles Mitchell, "Benjamin West's 'Death of General Wolfe' and the Popular History Piece," p. 20.

22. A reduced version of the painting on wood panel is thought to be by West and may have been done as a model for the reproductive print. That version recently appeared in the marketplace and was sold to a private collection through Phillips Auctioneers, New York, November 28, 2000, lot 7.

23. See Vivien Green Fryd, "Rereading the Indian in Benjamin West's *Death of General Wolfe*," *American Art* 9 (Spring 1995): 80.

24. For details of Spenser's biography, I have relied extensively on a variety of published sources. See especially, Elizabeth Heale's introduction to *The Faerie Queene: A Reader's Guide* (Cambridge: Cambridge University Press, 1987), pp. 1–11. The biography and timeline in "The Edmund Spenser Home Page," http://www.english.cam.ac.uk/spenser/biography.htm, also proved useful.

25. More on the representation of Elizabeth in Spenser, and in British portraiture more broadly, can be found in Annette Dixon, ed., *Women Who Ruled: Queens, Goddesses, Amazons in Renaissance and Baroque Art* (London: Merrell, in Association with the University of Michigan Museum of Art, 2002), esp. pp. 136–43.

26. Quoted in Edwin Greenlaw, Charles Grosvenor Osgood, and Frederick Morgan Padelford, eds., *The Works of Edmund Spenser: A Variorum Edition, The Faerie Queene, Book One* (Baltimore: The Johns Hopkins Press, 1932), p. 168. All quotations from *The Faerie Queene* are taken from this source.

27. Susan Doran, *Queen Elizabeth I* (New York: New York University Press, 2003), p. 124.

28. Richard Frushell identifies 318 such works in his study, *Edmund Spenser in the Eighteenth Century: Education, Imitation, and the Making of a Literary Model* (Pittsburgh: Dusquesne University Press, 1999), p. 1. One important contribution to this vogue for emulating the sixteenth-century poet was the popular work *A Canto of the Fairy Queen, Written by Spenser, Never before published* (1739), written by Gilbert West. That long imitative poem drew contemporary praise from Horace Walpole, among others. Frushell, p. 238.

29. For a full discussion of the phenomenon, see Christine Gerrard, "Political Elizabethanism and the Spenser Revival," in *The Patriot Opposition to Walpole: Politics, Poetry, and the National Myth*, 1725–1742 (Oxford: Clarendon Press, 1994), pp. 150–84, esp. 166–69.

30. See Andrew Hadfield, "William Kent's Illustrations of the Faerie Queene," *Spenser Studies: A Renaissance Poetry Annual* 14 (2000): 8.

31. Helmut von Erffa speculated that West first came to know Spenser through the library of such a British gentleman, Topham Beauclerk. See von Erffa, "Benjamin West: The Early Years in London," *American Art Journal* 5 (November 1973): 7.

32. Thomas Warton, *Observations on the Fairy Queen of Spenser*, 2 vols. (London: R. Dutton and Thomas Ostell, 1820). According to twentieth-century academics, "critical study of Spenser began early in the eighteenth century and has continued without interruption to our own day. The eighteenth century editors and commentators, though inclined to take undue liberties with the text, and though somewhat influenced by 'classical' standards, laid a substantial foundation of scholarship, especially in showing the indebtedness of the poet to classical writers, to the medieval romances, and to the Italian poets." C[harles] G[rovesnor] O[sgood] and F[rederick] M[organ] P[adelford], preface to *The Works of Edmund Spenser*, v.

33. Warton, sec. 1, 1762, quoted in Frushell, *Edmund Spenser in the Eighteenth Century*, pp. 127–28.

34. These volumes, edited by Thomas Birch, are included in the exhibition. *The Faerie Queene* (London: J. Brindley and S. Wright, 1751). See Hadfield, "William Kent's Illustrations," p. 6.

35. Because Kent died in 1748, three years before the text was published, he may not have finished all of the illustrations planned for the volume. His reading of the text, like West's and others', concentrated on the first book because it was known best at the time. See Hadfield, "William Kent's Illustrations," p. 8.

36. In a letter to a Montagu, dated June 13, 1751, Walpole complained: "The first volume of Spenser is published with prints designed by Kent; but the most execrable performance you ever beheld—the graving not worse than the drawing: awkward knights, scrambling Unas, hills tumbling down themselves, no variety of prospect, and three or four perpetual spruce firs." Quoted in Allen T. Hazen, *A Catalogue of Horace Walpole's Library* (New Haven: Yale University Press, 1969), 1:323.

37. Horace Walpole, *Anecdotes of Painting in England* (1826; reprint, New York: Anno Press, 1969), 3:59–60.

38. Joseph Warton, *An Essay on the Genius and Writings of Pope* (London, 1764), 1:219, quoted in Renate Prochno, "Nationalism in British Eighteenth-Century Painting: Sir Joshua Reynolds and Benjamin West," in *Nationalism in the Visual Arts*, ed. Richard R. Etlin (Washington, D.C.: National Gallery of Art, 1991), p. 28.

39. See Robert D. Altick, *Painting from Books: Art and Literature in Britain, 1760–1900* (Columbus: The Ohio State University Press, 1985), p. 346.

40. Ibid. The other essential sources documenting the popularity of Spenser for artists of this period are Norman K. Farmer, Jr., "'A Moniment Forever More': *The Faerie Queene* in British Art 1770–1950," *Princeton University Library Chronicle* 52 (Autumn 1990): 25–77; and Laurel Bradley, "Eighteenth-Century Paintings and Illustrations of Spenser's Faerie Queene: A Study in Taste," *Marsyas: Studies in the History of Art* 22 (1979–1980): 31–51.

41. On the iconological significance of the donkey, a traditional symbol of the Church, see J. M. Steadman, "Una and the Clergy: The Ass Symbol in the Faerie Queene," *Journal of the Warburg and Courtauld Institutes* 21 (1958): 131–37.

42. See von Erffa and Staley, *The Paintings of Benjamin West*, pp. 277–78.

43. This passage was reproduced in the *Middlesex Journal* 480 (April 25–28, 1772), as quoted in von Erffa and Staley, *The Paintings of Benjamin West*.

44. Quoted in Elizabeth Mankin Kornhauser's entry on the picture in *American Painting Before 1945 in the Wadsworth Atheneum* (New Haven: Yale University Press, 1996), 2:782–84.

45. See von Erffa and Staley, *The Paintings of Benjamin West*, p. 278.

46. David Lubin's reading of John Vanderlyn's painting *Ariadne Asleep on the Island of Naxos*, while it does not connect this work directly back to West as a precursor, could be extended to this end. See his "Labyrinths of Meaning in Vanderlyn's Ariadne," in *Picturing a Nation: Art and Politics in Nineteenth-Century America* (New Haven: Yale University Press, 1994), pp. 1–53, esp. 5–47.

47. Two painted versions of *The Cave of Despair* exist. One is in the Duxbury Art Center in Duxbury, Massachusetts, and the other is in the Yale Center for British Art in New Haven, Connecticut. Yale's picture is generally assumed to be the first of these two works, with Duxbury's being a later copy by the artist. See curatorial files at the Yale Center for British Art for documents that make a case for this chronology.

48. See, for example, Warton, *Observations on the Fairy Queen of Spenser*, 2:24–25.

49. *Cave of Despaire* appears as plate X in *The Gallery of Pictures Painted By Benjamin West, Esqr., first painter to His Majesty & President of the Royal Academy engraved in outline by Henry Moses* (London, 1811); Turner's letter to Charles Eastlake, dated August 11, 1829, is quoted in von Erffa and Staley, *The Paintings of Benjamin West*, p. 279.

50. We have already seen that he was familiar with the Englishman's writing from as early as 1863, when still in Venice, he created an illustration of *Savage Warrior Taking Leave of His Family* for the Italian translation of Burke's *Account of European Settlements in America*; von Erffa and Staley, *The Paintings of Benjamin West*, p. 62.

51. See Alberts, *Benjamin West: A Biography*, p. 214.

52. Most relevant for our study, on April 19, 1774, Burke delivered his speech "On American Taxation," which was quickly published and reprinted by Benjamin Towne in Philadelphia by 1775. In 1780 Burke published *An Impartial History of the War in America, between Great Britain and her colonies, from its commencement to the end of the year 1779*. In March 1775 he delivered his "Speech on Conciliation with America," which argued "to restore order and repose to an empire so great and so distracted as ours." Burke was born in Dublin, Ireland, but rose to a position of intellectual prominence in England. West would have felt strong sympathy with both his words and his personal background.

53. More than just coincidental resemblance can be detected in a comparison of the figures in this painting's middle ground and Kent's treatment of Una and Redcrosse in his illustrations. See, in particular, plates 11 and 14 for possible sources. It may be that West looked at other printed precedents for elements used in his *Faerie Queene* series. William Hogarth designed engravings for an English-language version of Cervantes's *Don Quixote* about 1726 which West may have consulted for the background of *Fidelia and Speranza* and as sources for *The Cave of Despair*. Ronald Paulson illustrates these works and provides an important discussion of British interpretative communities for Cervantes in his *Don Quixote in England: The Aesthetics of Laughter* (Baltimore: Johns Hopkins University Press, 1998).

54. The impressive formal qualities of this work and the meaning of the attributes have been discussed in Michael Quick's entry on the picture in *Timken Museum of Art: European Works of Art, American Paintings, and Russian Icons in the Putnam Foundation Collection* (San Diego: Timken Museum of Art, 1996), pp. 206–9.

55. A small ink drawing, probably done after the painting was finished, shows a more cheerful image of Fidelia, thus following the text still more precisely. That work was sold at a Sotheby Parke-Bernet auction in London on March 22, 1979, as lot 6, and is now unlocated.

56. Von Erffa and Staley have noted the resemblance between the two works and speculate that the exhibition of *Fidelia and Speranza* at the Royal Academy in 1777 may have inspired the commission. See their entry on the Dundas double portrait, no. 612, in their *The Paintings of Benjamin West*, pp. 502–3.

57. Von Erffa and Staley devote considerable space in their catalogue raisonné to disputing the identities of the National Gallery's attributions for this work, as well as its dating. See their entry, no. 647, and their lengthy discussion, ibid., pp. 523–24.

58. William Empson, *Seven Kinds of Ambiguity* (New York: New Directions, 1947), pp. 123–24.

59. Helmut von Erffa, "Benjamin West at the Height of His Career," *American Art Journal* 1 (Spring 1969): 19.

60. The most articulate advocate of this allegorical understanding has been Stephen Greenblatt, whose discussion of the Guyon and the Bower of Bliss episode as a commentary on New World Utopias provides a central part of his argument in *Renaissance Self-Fashioning: From More to Shakespeare* (Chicago: University of Chicago Press, 1980), pp. 179–82. Recently, David Read has questioned the narrowness of Greenblatt's new historicist interpretation of book 2, while not disputing the overall value of interpretations that connect *The Faerie Queene* to New World knowledge. See Read's challenging book, *Temperate Conquests: Spenser in the Spanish New World* (Detroit: Wayne State University Press, 2002).

61. See Wendy Greenhouse, "Benjamin West and Edward III: A Neoclassical Painter and Medieval History," *Art History* 8 (June 1985): 176–91, for an account of some of these works. A discussion of George III's motives for associating his reign to medieval ideals, especially as this relates to commissions by West, can be found in David Watkins, "George III and the Shift to Gothic: An Essay in Nationalism," in *New Offerings: Ancient Treasures: Studies in Medieval Art for George Henderson* (London: Stroud, Sutton, 2001), pp. 519–36.

62. All three of the subjects depicted by West in his series are represented in Crane's text. Crane was the text's most profuse illustrator by far, however. See *Walter Crane's Illustrations and Ornamentation from the Faerie Queene* (Mineola, N.Y.: Dover Publications, 1999), pp. 6, 14, 15.

63. Charles Grosvenor Osgood, *The Glory 'Round About* (Baltimore: Enoch Pratt Free Library, 1945), p. 11. Osgood spoke with authority on Spenser. He was an Elizabethan literary scholar and one of three editors of Variorum edition of *The Works of Edmund Spenser.*

Catalogue of the Exhibition

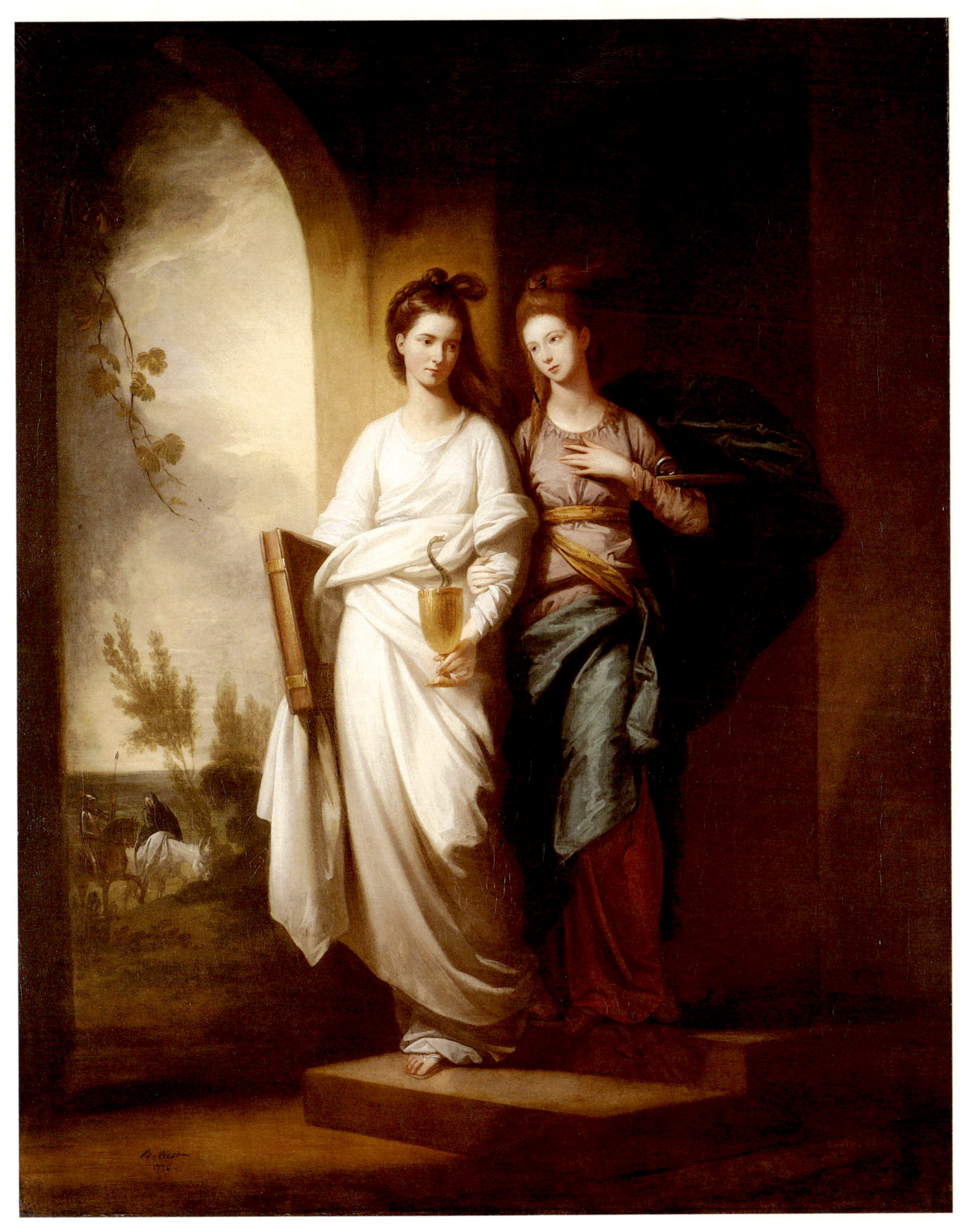

CATALOGUE 1

Benjamin West, *Fidelia and Speranza,* 1776

Oil on canvas, 53¾ x 42⅝ in.

The Putnam Foundation, Timken Museum of Art

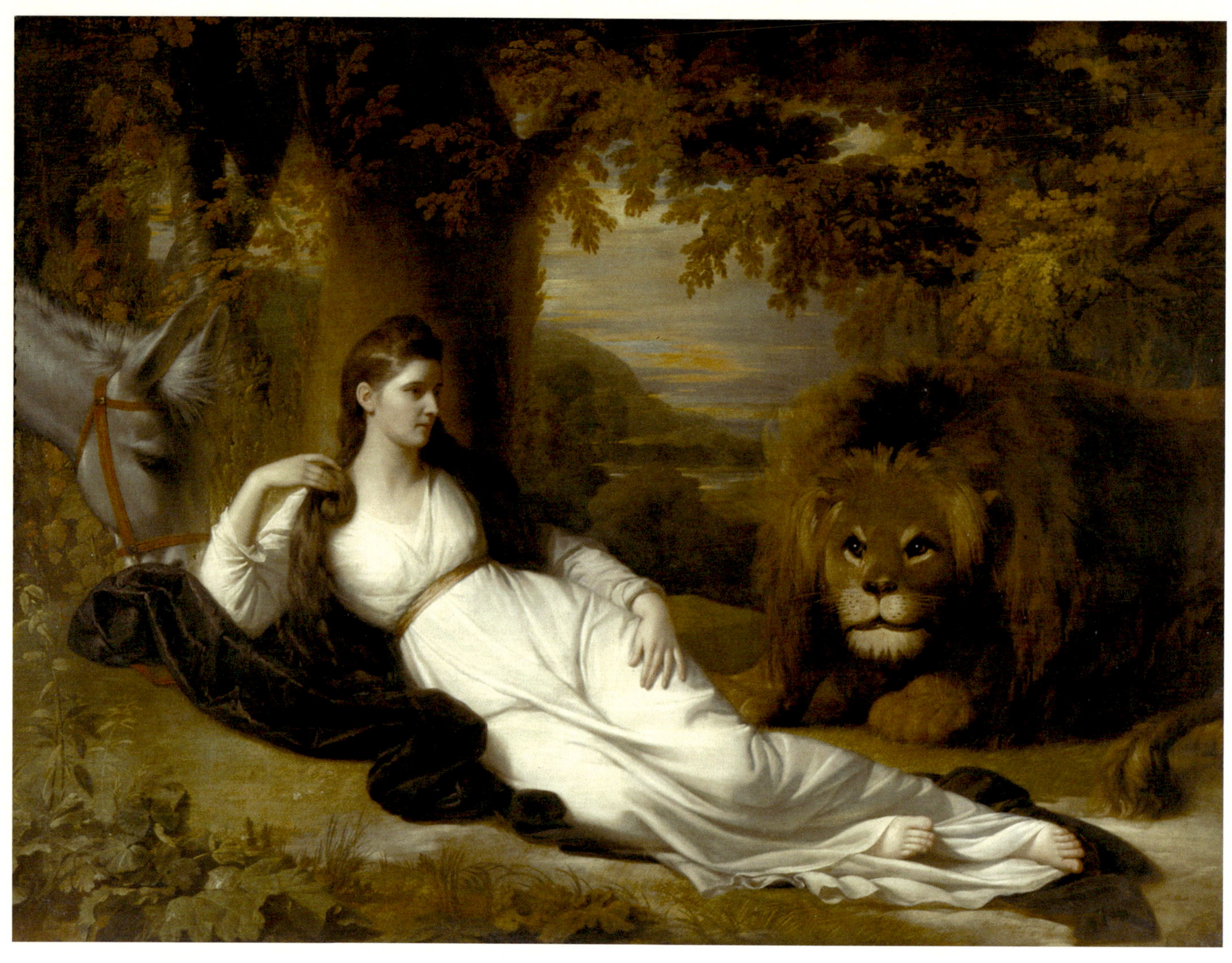

CATALOGUE 2

Benjamin West, *Una and the Lion,* 1771

Oil on canvas, 66¼ x 86⅛ in.

Wadsworth Atheneum Museum of Art, Hartford, Connecticut. The Ella Gallup Sumner and Mary Catlin Sumner Collection Fund, 1941.591

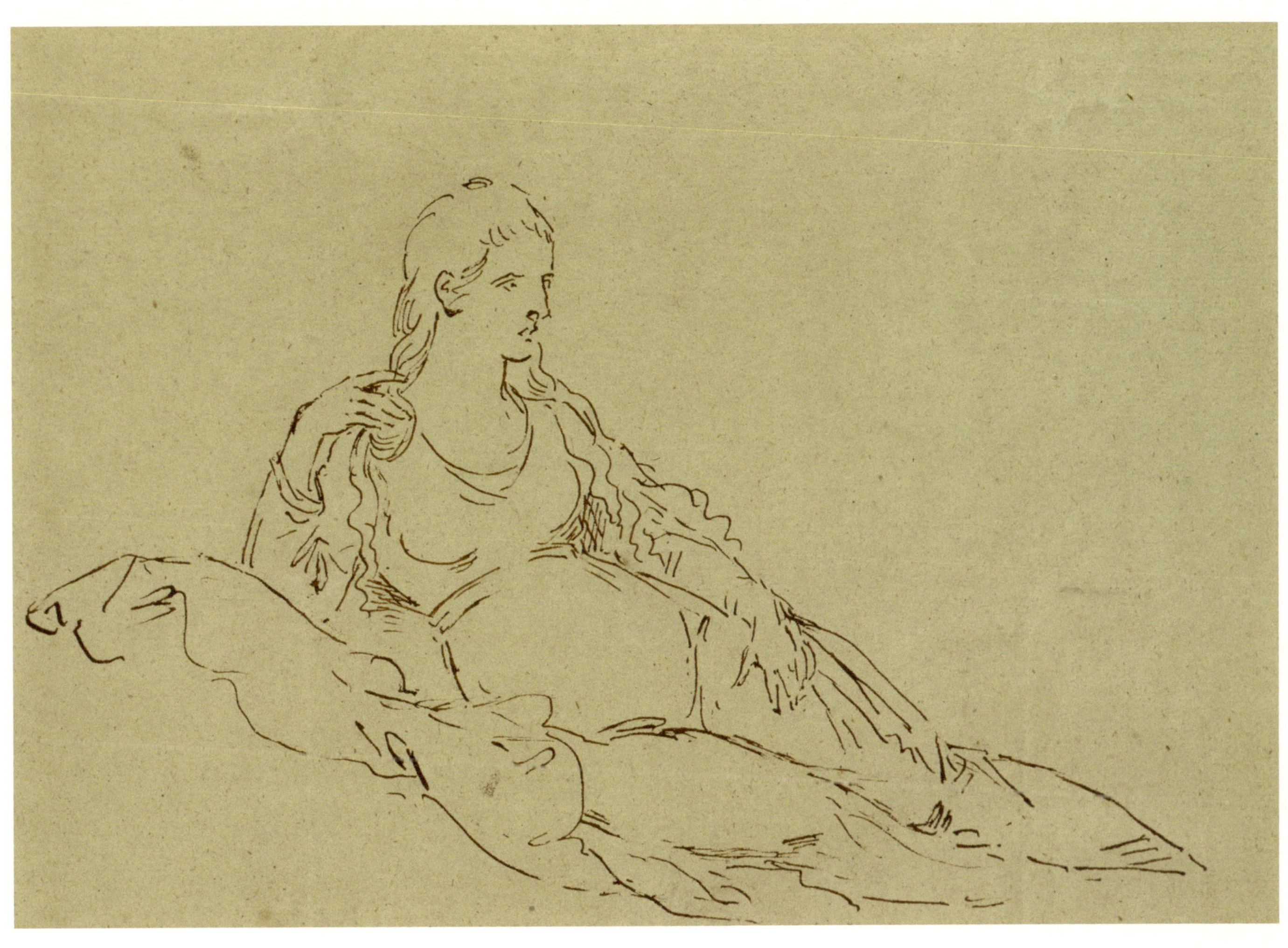

CATALOGUE 3

Benjamin West, *Una,* c. 1771

Pen and ink on paper, 10¼ x 12½ in.

Wadsworth Atheneum Museum of Art, Hartford, Connecticut.
Purchased of Bernard Black Gallery from Keney Fund, 1968.89

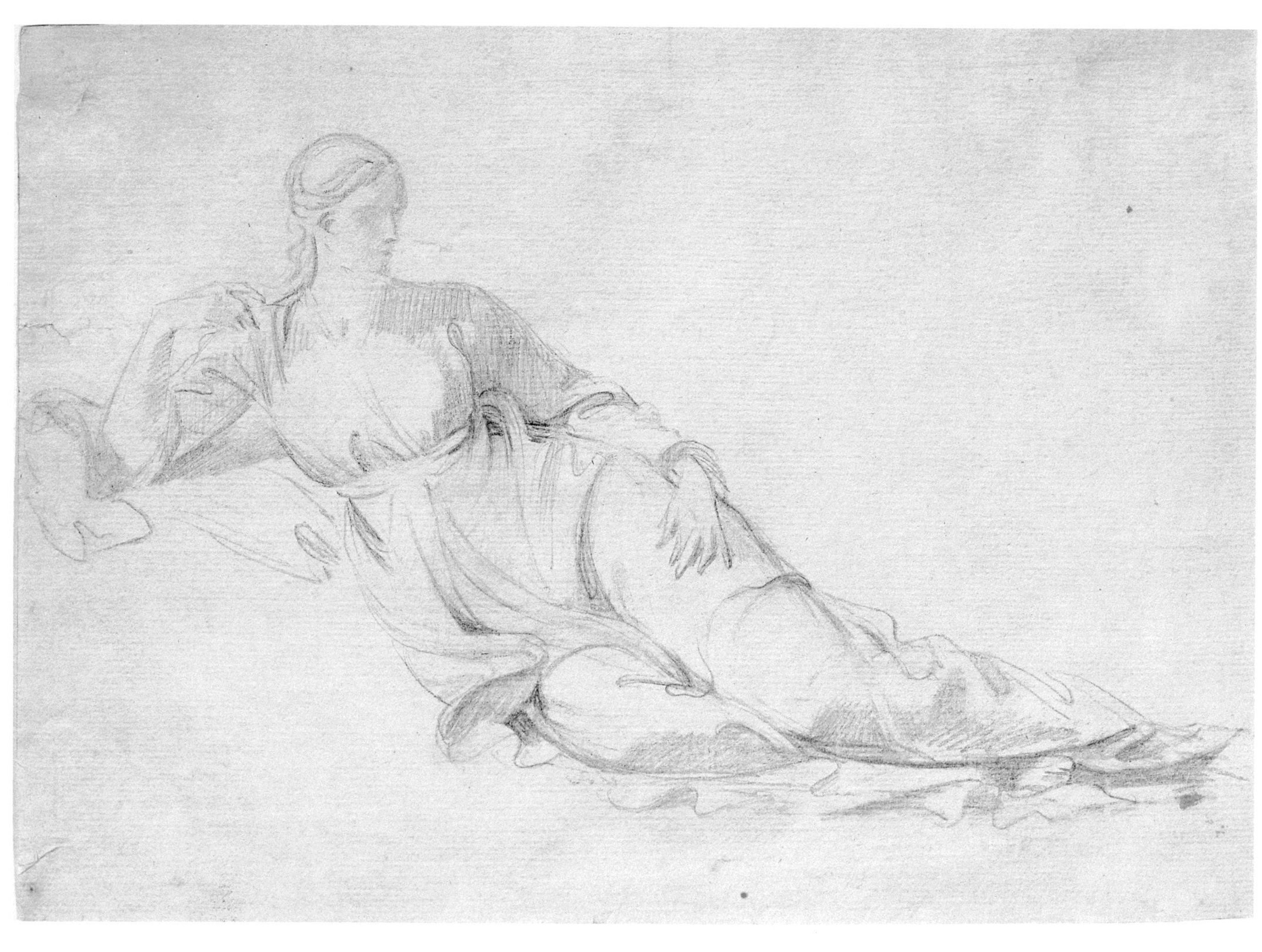

CATALOGUE 4

Benjamin West, *Una,* c. 1771

Graphite on paper, 6⅝ x 9 in.

Friends Historical Library, Swarthmore College, Swarthmore, Pennsylvania

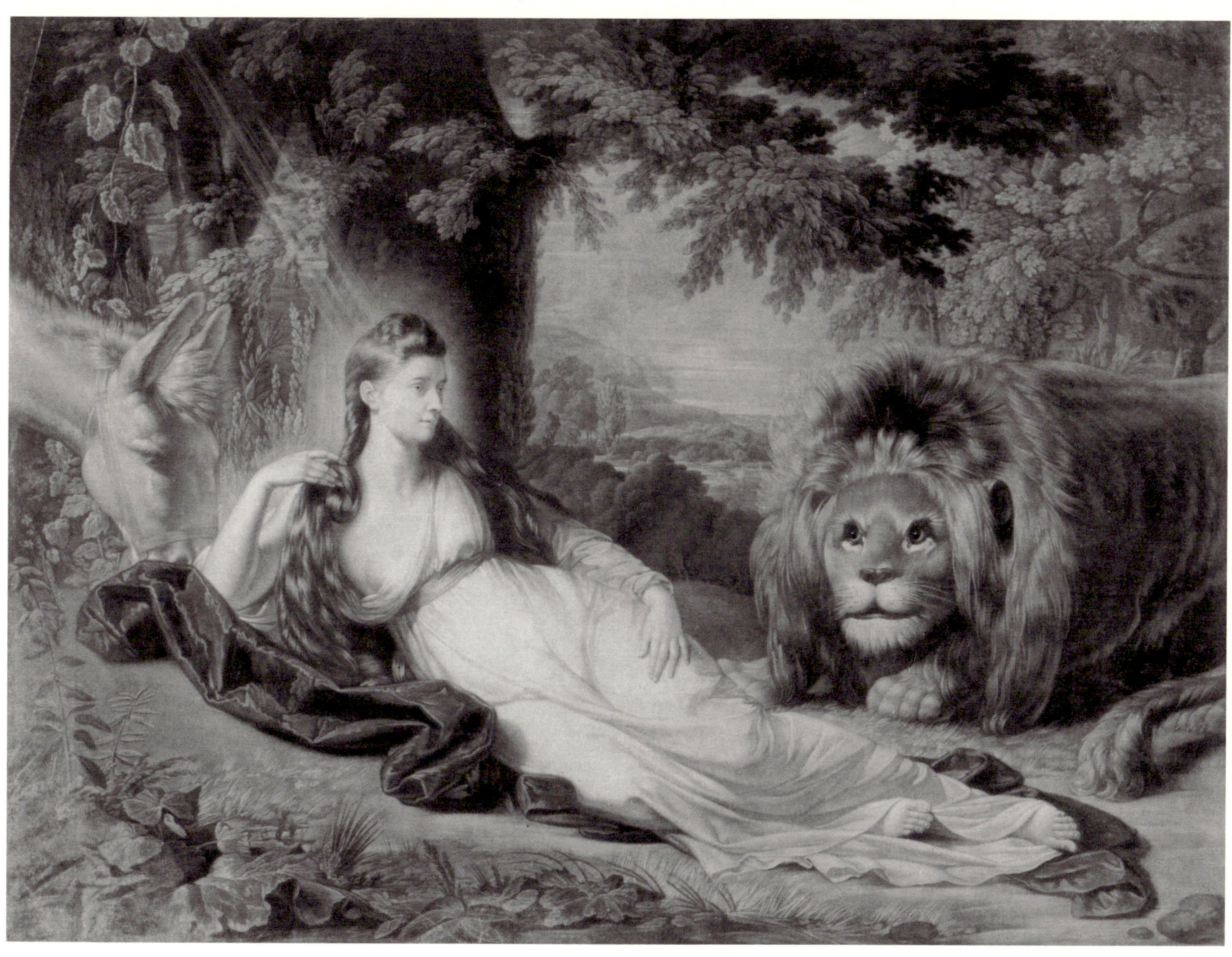

CATALOGUE 5

Benjamin West, *Una and the Lion,* published 1772

Mezzotint, 18 11/16 x 23 3/8 in.

Hood Museum of Art, Dartmouth College, Hanover, New Hampshire; purchased through a gift from the Estate of Russell Cowles, Class of 1909, PR 2004.11.

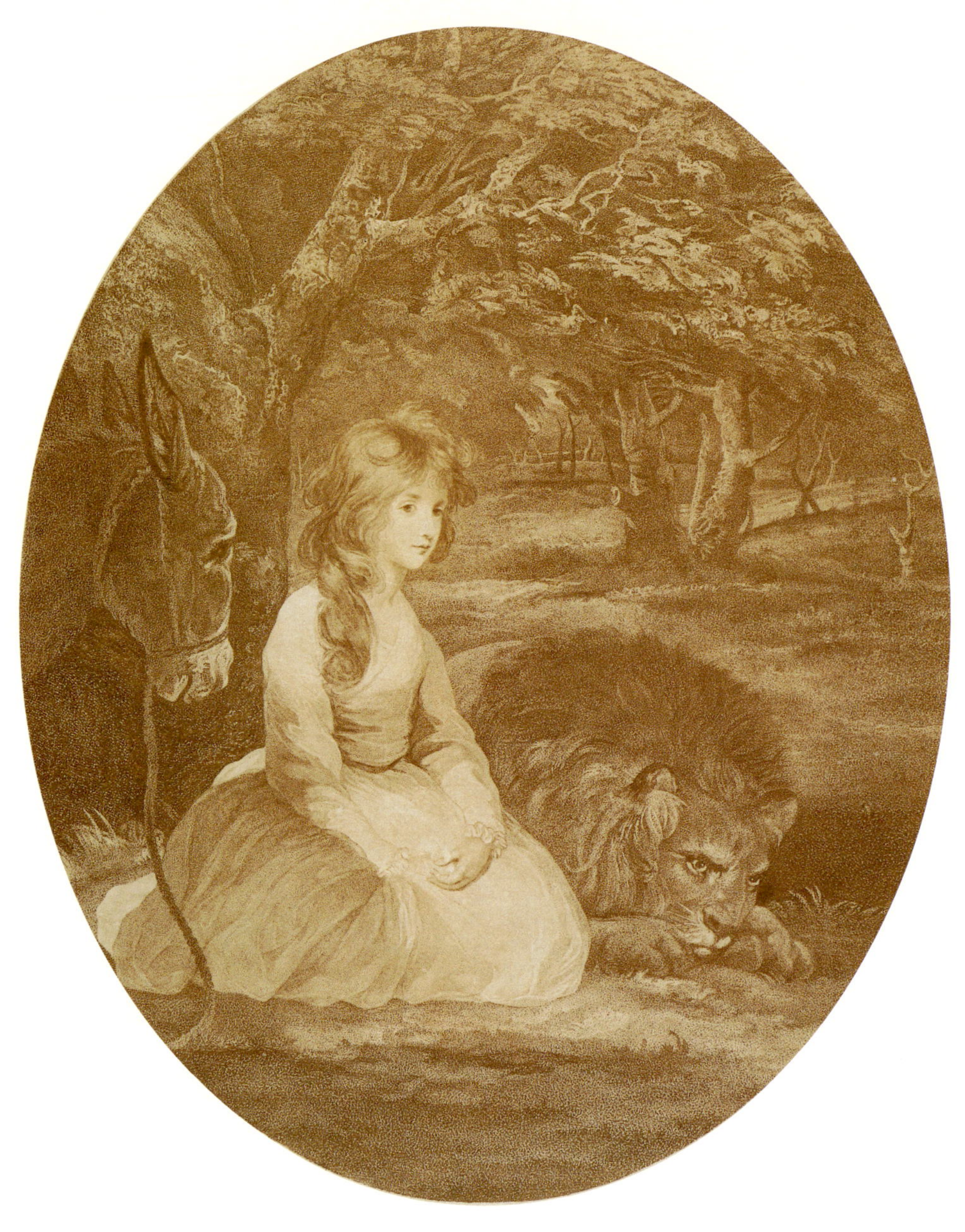

CATALOGUE 6

Thomas Watson after Sir Joshua Reynolds, *Miss Elizabeth Beauclerc as Una*

Etched stipple, 12 7/16 x 10 in. (oval)

Yale Center for British Art, Gift of Mr. and Mrs. Leon Korn, B1980.17.1

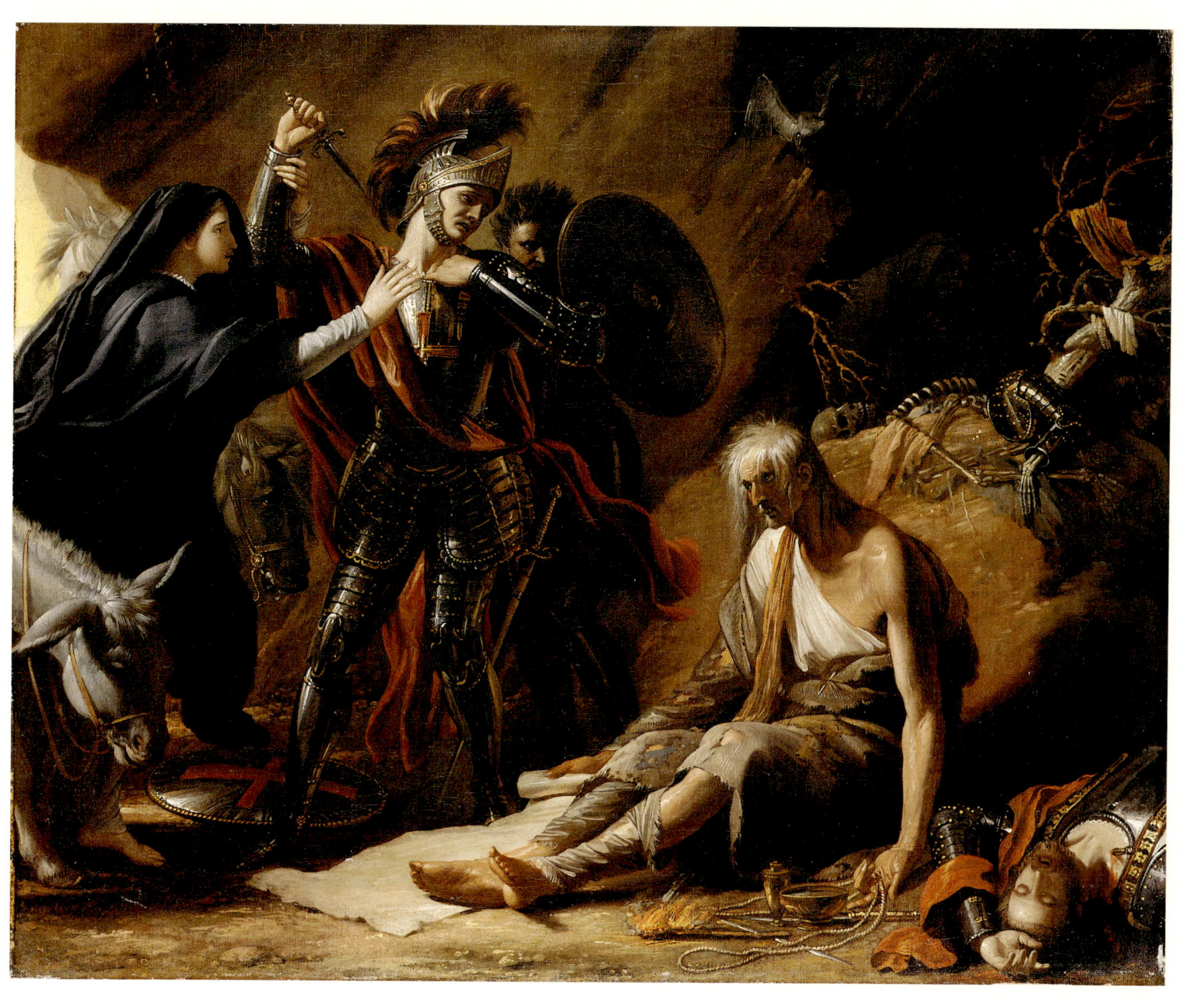

CATALOGUE 7

Benjamin West, *The Cave of Despair,* 1772
Oil on canvas, 24 x 30 in.

Yale Center for British Art, Paul Mellon Collection, B1977.14.113

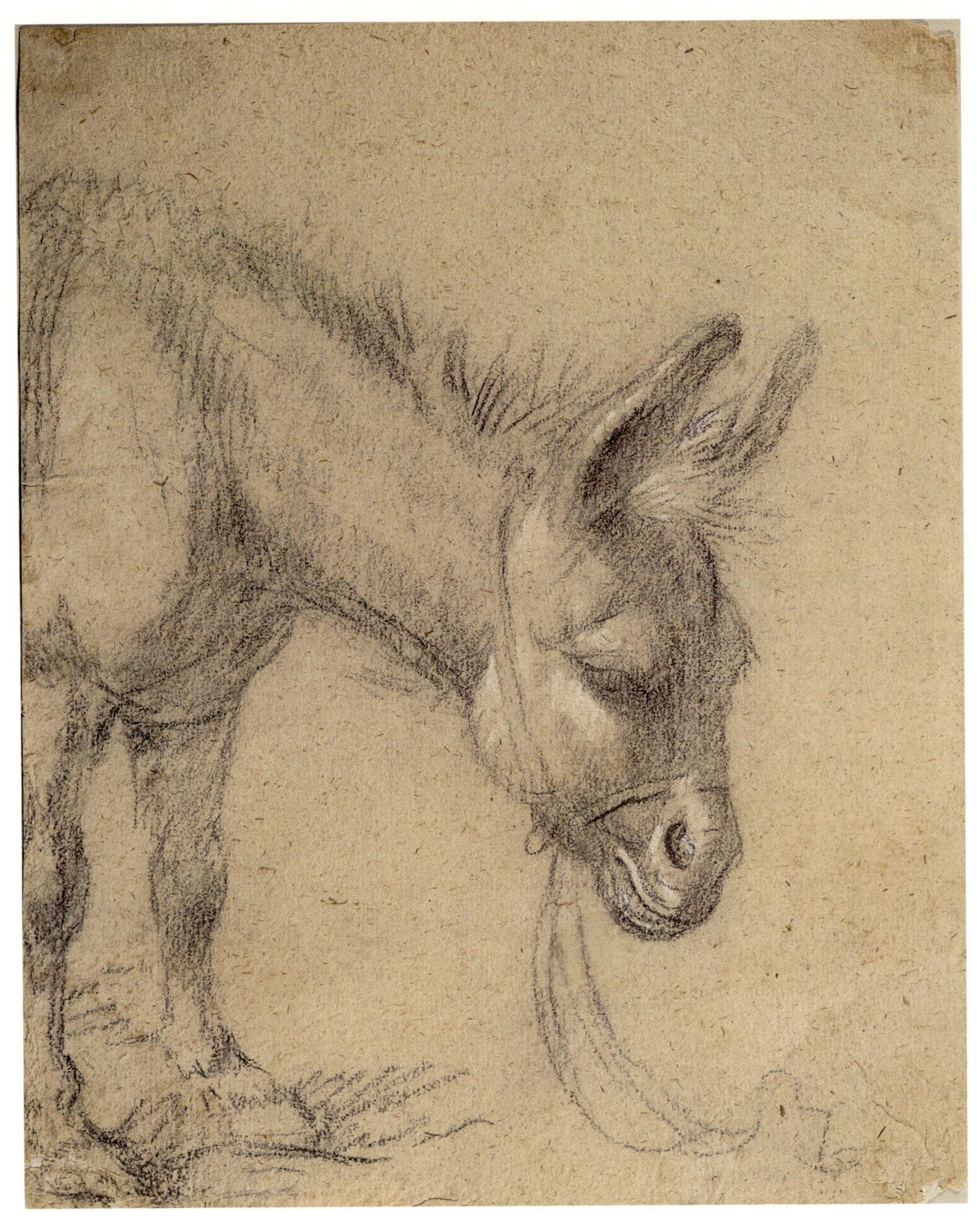

CATALOGUE 8

Benjamin West, *Donkey's Head (Study for "Una and the Lion")*, c. 1771
Black and white chalk on paper, 10⅝ x 8⅜ in.

Friends Historical Library, Swarthmore College, Swarthmore, Pennsylvania

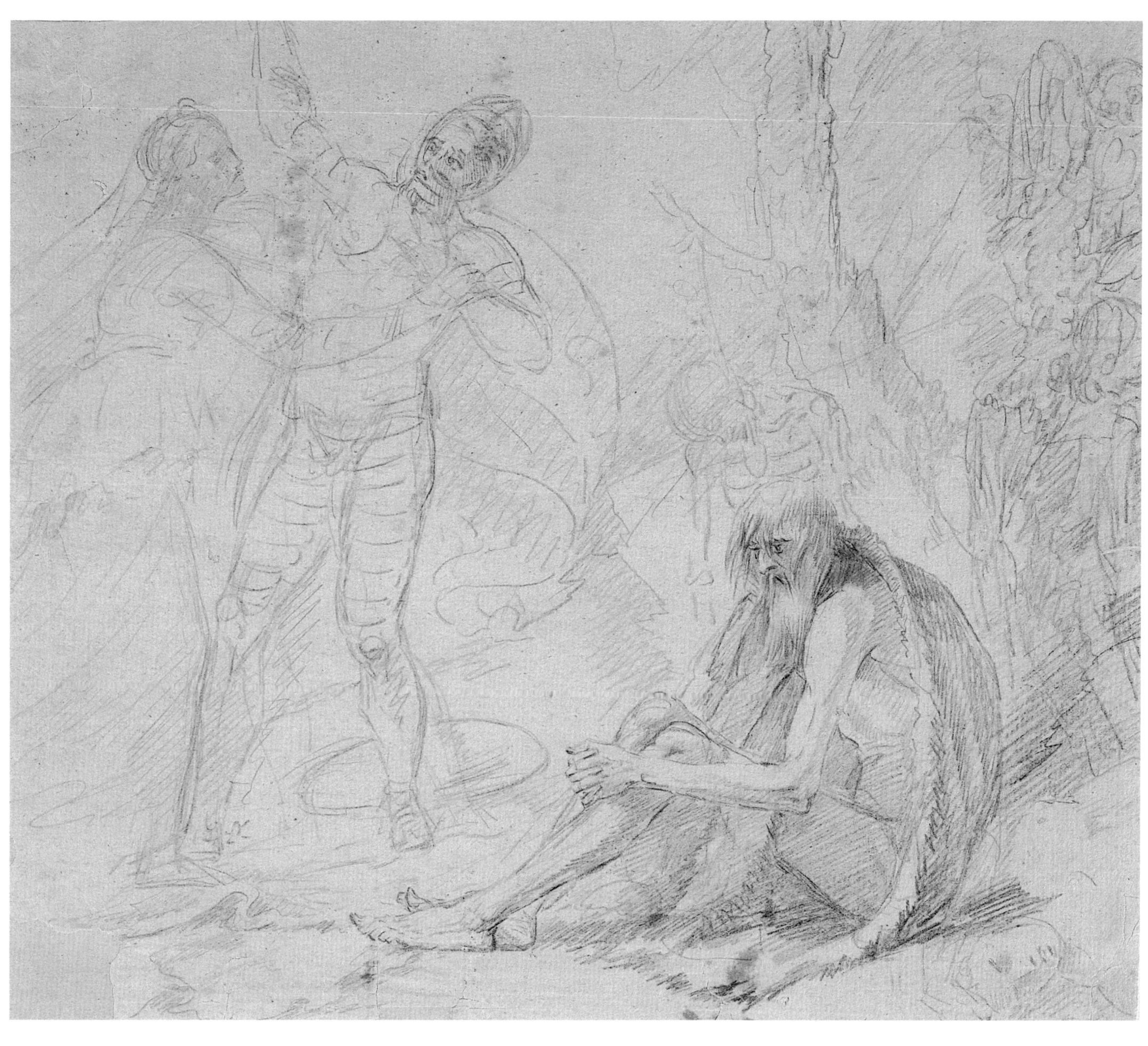

CATALOGUE 9

Benjamin West, *Studies for "The Cave of Despair"*
Black chalk on paper, 10⅛ x 11¼ in.

Friends Historical Library, Swarthmore College, Swarthmore, Pennsylvania

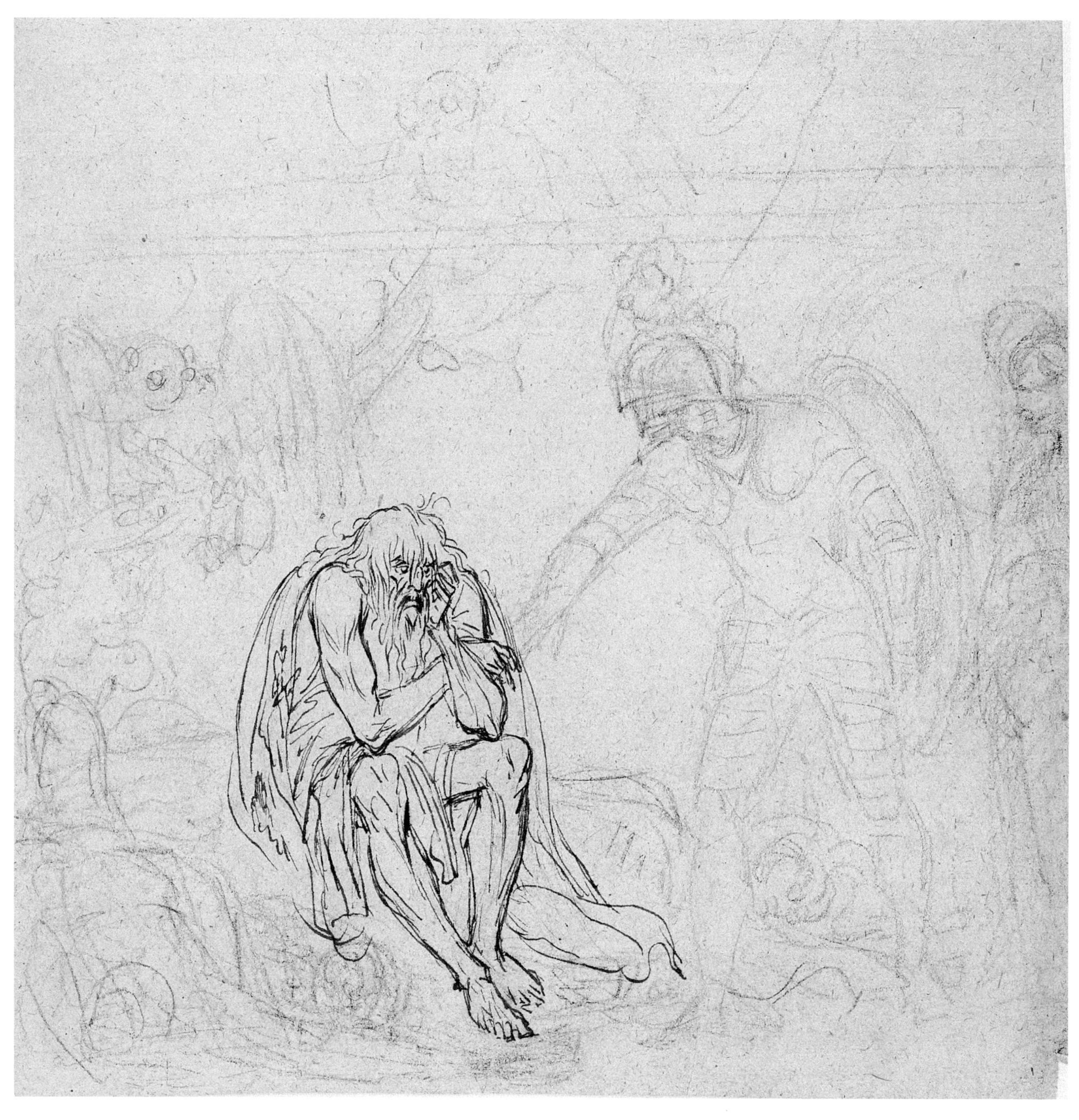

CATALOGUE 10

Benjamin West, *Study for "The Cave of Despair,"* c. 1772
Ink and graphite on paper, 10½ x 8$^{1}/_{16}$ in.

Montreal Museum of Fine Arts, Purchase, Mr. and Mrs. Gerald Bronfman Fund for Master Graphics, Dr. 1967.207. Photo: Christine Guest